ROUTLEDGE LIBRARY EDITIONS: NUCLEAR SECURITY

Volume 16

INTERNATIONAL ATOMIC POLICY DURING A DECADE

INTERNATIONAL ATOMIC POLICY DURING A DECADE

An Historical-Political Investigation into the Problem of Atomic Weapons During the Period 1945–55

ELIS BIÖRKLUND

Routledge
Taylor & Francis Group
LONDON AND NEW YORK

First published in 1956 by George Allen & Unwin Ltd

This edition first published in 2021
by Routledge
2 Park Square, Milton Park, Abingdon, Oxon OX14 4RN

and by Routledge
52 Vanderbilt Avenue, New York, NY 10017

Routledge is an imprint of the Taylor & Francis Group, an informa business

© 1956 Admiral Elis Biörklund

All rights reserved. No part of this book may be reprinted or reproduced or utilised in any form or by any electronic, mechanical, or other means, now known or hereafter invented, including photocopying and recording, or in any information storage or retrieval system, without permission in writing from the publishers.

Trademark notice: Product or corporate names may be trademarks or registered trademarks, and are used only for identification and explanation without intent to infringe.

British Library Cataloguing in Publication Data
A catalogue record for this book is available from the British Library

ISBN: 978-0-367-50682-7 (Set)
ISBN: 978-1-00-309763-1 (Set) (ebk)
ISBN: 978-0-367-53797-5 (Volume 16) (hbk)
ISBN: 978-1-00-308337-5 (Volume 16) (ebk)

Publisher's Note
The publisher has gone to great lengths to ensure the quality of this reprint but points out that some imperfections in the original copies may be apparent.

Disclaimer
The publisher has made every effort to trace copyright holders and would welcome correspondence from those they have been unable to trace.

INTERNATIONAL ATOMIC POLICY

DURING A DECADE

*An historical-political investigation
into the problem of atomic weapons
during the period 1945-55*

by

Admiral ELIS BIÖRKLUND

Translated in Stockholm by
ALBERT READ
*in co-operation with the author.
The text has been brought up to date
to June 1955*

LONDON
GEORGE ALLEN & UNWIN LTD
RUSKIN HOUSE · MUSEUM STREET

FIRST PUBLISHED IN 1956

This book is copyright under the Berne Convention. Apart from any fair dealing for the purposes of private study, research, criticism or review, as permitted under the Copyright Act 1911, no portion may be reproduced by any process without written permission. Enquiry should be made to the publisher

*Printed in Great Britain
in 11 on 12 Monotype Baskerville type
by The Shenval Press, Simson Shand Ltd.,
London, Hertford and Harlow.*

CONTENTS

	PAGE
Preface	9

CHAPTER

1 FUNDAMENTALS   13

2 THE POST-WAR PERIOD 1945–50   18
   Political Survey 1945–50
   Conference Problems 1946–48
   Conference Problems and Certain Scientific Problems 1949–50

3 THE HYDROGEN BOMB PERIOD 1951–55   29
   The Political Situation 1951. No Conferences
   The Political Situation 1952
   Conference Problems 1952
   The Political Situation 1953
   Conference Problems 1953
   The Political Situation 1954–55
   Conference Problems 1954–55

4 THE PROBLEM FROM THE VIEWPOINT OF THE WESTERN POWERS   43
   USA 1945–50
   USA 1951–52
   USA 1953
   USA 1954–55

CHAPTER		PAGE
	Western Europe	58
	The Western European Union	
	Great Britain	
	France	
	Belgium	
	The Supreme Organization of the Western Powers	
5	THE PROBLEM FROM THE VIEWPOINT OF THE EASTERN POWERS	67
	Soviet 1945–50	
	Soviet 1951–52	
	Soviet 1953	
	Soviet 1954–55	
	The Satellite States	
	The People's Republic of China	
	The Supreme Organization of the Eastern Powers	
6	THE TECHNICAL DEVELOPMENT OF ATOMIC WEAPONS	96
7	THE POSSIBILITY OF INTERNATIONAL CONTROL	100
8	LIMITATION OF ALL ATOMIC WEAPONS OR ONLY LARGE ONES?	105
9	ABSOLUTE OR CONDITIONAL PROHIBITION OF USE?	108

CHAPTER	PAGE
10 BIOLOGICAL AND CHEMICAL WEAPONS	111
11 ROBOT WEAPONS	114
12 THE CONNECTION BETWEEN ABC WEAPONS AND CONVENTIONAL ARMAMENTS	116
13 ATOMIC ENERGY IN PEACE AND WAR	120
14 SUMMARY	123
Appendix 1 *Sources*	133
Appendix 2 *Important Deposits of Fissionable Material*	142
Appendix 3 *Map of Sources of Raw Materials*	facing page 148

PREFACE

In all countries it is agreed that one of the most serious and difficult problems in world affairs is the situation in which the development of atomic weapons has placed us. Where is it leading us? Is it possible to come to an acceptable solution, or must humanity be driven aimlessly along by newly discovered forces of nature towards a future filled with the fear of the destruction of civilization? These are the thoughts that occupy the minds of enlightened people, and throw a black shadow of pessimism over the future.

During my military career I took part in the great disarmament conferences of the 1920's and 30's, and having a knowledge of English, French, German and Russian, I became deeply interested in the political problems lying on the boundary between the foreign policies of the great powers and the upper strata of military-strategic conceptions. A study of world literature deepened my interest in this 'border area', which is so seldom touched upon in literature, and a number of articles were published, particularly on the relatively unknown Soviet Union, a country that I have studied for the past forty years or so. But atomic problems began to occupy a greater part of the discussion of the reduction of tension, further complicated by the political situation—extremely involved even before the advent of atomic problems—and inspired me to study the atomic question.

It is already several years since I came to the conclusion that the political antagonism between a democratic way of life and the theory of Soviet-Communism is so great that tension can only be reduced in stages as mutual mistrust is diminished. I have never had any confidence in the argument that military disarmament could be achieved in order to attain in this way a reduction of tension. On the contrary, experience has shown that a reduction of political stress is a necessary prelude to a decrease in armaments.

But the rapid development of atomic weapons made the problem still more complicated and seemingly impossible to solve. In spite of that, I felt an inner urge to try to make some small contribution towards a solution of the great military-political problems of the world, about which I had long been writing articles. During 1954 articles were published in *New York Times* and *Revue des deux Mondes*.

I also began outlining the various solutions of the problems of the limitation of atomic weapons, international control and prohibition, which I was able to find out by the study of the reports of all the international conferences dealing with such matters (see page 131-2). This made necessary a special study of the question of control, and that led to an extensive investigation into how the world's deposits of fissionable material, uranium and others, were distributed.

A table of the world's uranium mines slowly took form (Appendix 2), and the map (Appendix 3), which should be opened out and consulted during the study of this book, was drawn. To establish permanent supervision of all these mines seemed to me quite impossible, and I was compelled to take the line of considerably reduced control, with suitable inspection.

An extensive study of the history of atomic policy, made with the support of Swedish State Council for Scientific Research, confirmed my conviction that if any results are

PREFACE

to be attained at all, we must aim at a realistic result.

A draft of this book showed that it is impossible to give a clear picture of such a complicated series of problems without first giving a survey of the situation in the world at the different points of time when international conferences dealt with these questions, and it struck me that nowhere in literature had I found a valuable work which dealt with the problems of atomic weapons with regard to their inseparable connection with contemporary international events during the decade ending with the close of 1954. Such a work had therefore to be written.

Then, but only then, is it possible with any hope of success to study in detail the internal relationship of each separate groups of powers. For problems of atomic weapons look very different from different points of view.

In order that the reader will be able to understand the elementary, technical atomic problems, technical information about the position of science in the various stages of development must be given. This made necessary a study of atomic science, which has been checked by very prominent scientists and technical specialists. The richest sources were, of course, the American 'International Bibliography on Atomic Energy', which contains information on 1,500 sources of both political and social interest (1), while the technical parts (2) of the same publication contain over 40,000 sources. The work of sifting the source material, of studying about 4,000 books and of obtaining many hundreds from abroad has been great, and later experience showed that only about 200 of them were of sufficient value to justify of their being included in the list of valuable sources (Appendix 1). In addition a large number of periodicals, particularly from the USA and Russia, had to be consulted. Political memoirs and the like, on the other hand, have not been included in the list of sources, which would then have swelled out to an unproportional degree.

On principle I have declined to make use of any but official sources, and those which are generally available. I have not performed the three years' research necessary in my capacity of officer, nor in any other official capacity, but as a private person deeply interested in the future of humanity. The book is not written for Scandinavian conditions, but for the world as a whole.

The ten-year period 1945–55 has been divided into two sections, partly because of technical reasons and partly because atomic problems during the post-war years 1945–50 were chiefly concerned with the atomic bomb, and the years 1951–55 with the hydrogen bomb.

ELIS BIÖRKLUND

Stockholm, May 1955

Chapter 1

FUNDAMENTALS

As this work is intended for the general reader and not for the expert, it has been deemed advisable to give a summary of events before the atomic bomb appeared on the scene, and to mention certain primary technical principles with which the reader must be familiar in order to understand what is said about the atomic bomb in Chapter 2. The same technical principles, as far as they refer to the hydrogen bomb, will be found at the end of Chapter 2 to help the reader to understand the following chapter.

According to Einstein's theory of 1905 (3), mass can be converted into energy and vice versa, and from a kilogramme of matter is should be possible to extract some millions of times more power than by the chemical combustion of one kilogramme of coal. It was only necessary to discover how to release these fantastic amounts of energy. The way of science to the solution of the problem was long and tedious, and will not be dealt with here. It is sufficient to say that nuclear physicists, such as E. Rutherford, as long ago as 1909 demonstrated that considerable amounts of energy could be obtained by splitting atoms, and in 1919 he was the first to split an atom.

Two German scientists, Hahn and Strassman, succeeded in 1938 in splitting uranium atoms, which Professor Bohr, the great Danish physicist, while travelling in the USA, told Einstein who, together with other scientists resident in America, wrote the letter to President Roosevelt which was the signal for the commencement of the great efforts made by America in the realm of nuclear physics. It is interesting to learn that *if Hitler had not been so uninterested in the discovery, it is quite possible that Germany would have had the atomic bomb before the USA*, with such terrifying results as can easily be imagined. *This brings us to the first serious, political observation regarding the enormous significance of the atomic bomb.*

The news of the German experiment spread through the world, and a large number of nuclear fissions were carried out in laboratories in several countries during the years 1939-40. The fundamental conception arrived at earlier was that the atom could be compared to a diminutive solar system with a nucleus and planets. Later the picture became more complicated, as will be shown below.

A nucleus consisting of positively charged particles, protons, is embedded in uncharged particles, called neutrons, so that externally the whole nucleus appears positively charged. The binding agents of the atomic nuclei are called mesons. Negatively charged electrons revolve round and at a relatively great distance from the nucleus, and their number is equal to the positive charge of the nucleus, so that outwardly the atom is electrically neutral, provided that it is not subjected to special external influence. It was discovered that the interior of the atom, particularly that of the nucleus, was kept together by very great forces. Fermi, an Italian scientist living in the USA, made a very important discovery in 1934, when he found a way of reducing the rapidity of the neutrons in their passage through hydrogenous substances, which facilitated nuclear reaction.

The number of positive charges was called the atomic number. It was found that the mass of the nucleus was always equal to an even multiple of the mass of the unit—a hydrogen atom—and this multiple was called the mass number. Two kinds of atoms with the same atomic num-

FUNDAMENTALS

ber but with different atomic weights were called isotopes. By 1940 scientists had progressed so far (4) that it was possible to work on the separation of isotopes of uranium (U 235), which element had, as early as 1938, been shown to be fissionable when bombarded with neutrons. Institutions were founded for the study of neutrons, and the hunt for uranium was begun. Experiments made at this time showed that when certain uranium isotopes were bombarded with neutrons, the uranium nucleus was split with enormous force, and the components ejected. The explosion was given the name fission.

It was also found that neutrons liberated from the nucleus split new atoms, so that a chain reaction was begun that had to be kept under control. In 1940 it was discovered that plutonium (Pu 239), an element obtained from U 238, could be split. In the autumn of 1939 President Roosevelt appointed a three-man committee to deal with questions pertaining to atoms, and in June 1940—at the same time as the European western front collapsed—the State made a grant towards atomic research. By June 1942, the first great organization had been created in the USA.

The American-British collaboration was augmented by scientists from several countries, but from 1943 onwards research work was localized wholly to the USA, partly on account of the war, partly for reasons of secrecy and partly from economic-financial considerations. Whole towns grew up in the USA regardless of cost, for the production of atomic energy, and the first atomic pile was created near Chicago in 1942. This project was kept secret, and placed under the charge of Fermi. By 1943 the USA had built up the atomic laboratory at Los Alamos in New Mexico, where Professor J. R. Oppenheimer led a staff of more than 500 specialists, 300 of whom were scientists.

INTERNATIONAL ATOMIC POLICY

The problem of the atomic bomb had been a subject of research in the USA since the summer of 1940. Several committees were formed and the organization grew rapidly; the available staff increased to 100,000. In the spring of 1943 military research was removed to the 'Manhattan Department' under General Groves, a plutonium factory was established and new laboratories grew up at Argonne, near Chicago, at Clinton in Tennessee, at Hanford on the Columbia River and at other places. The electro-magnetic method of separating isotopes gained ground, and from 1944 Uranium 235 of sufficient enrichment for use in atomic bombs was produced. Other methods of separation used were those of gaseous and thermal diffusion. The most difficult problem attached to the manufacture of atomic bombs was that the explosion started too slowly and that the parts flew apart too fast for the explosion really to get properly under way. It was further realized that there was a critical size for the unit of chain reaction, and theoretical calculations and practical experiments had to be made in collaboration with each other.

The first bomb test was made at Trinity Site, near Alamogordo, New Mexico, at the beginning of July 1945. Up to May 1945 there was much anxiety in the USA that Germany would be first with the atomic bomb, and the work was urged forward with great energy. The first bomb was exploded from a tower, not dropped from an aeroplane. The effect was extremely impressive, and the difficulties of using the bomb from aeroplanes were soon overcome. On August 6, 1945, the second bomb—the Hiroshima Bomb, which lent its name to the atomic bomb—was dropped. The Soviet Union had promised at the Yalta Conference to take part in the war against Japan in the near future, and declared war on August 8; thus

Russia was able to take advantage of the opportunity of sharing the fruits of victory. The third atomic bomb was dropped on Nagasaki on August 9. President Truman and Mr Attlee, the Prime Minister of Britain, published their declaration on the aim of the atomic bomb, and Japan capitulated on August 10. It should be observed that the Western Powers suspected that Germany had atomic bombs in reserve for use in a desperate situation—but the American Government knew by their information services that this danger was not great—and that Germany surrendered at the beginning of May, before the bombs were dropped on Japan.

In December it was decided, with the concurrence of Russia, to establish an international commission to consider questions of atomic energy.

Chapter 2

THE POST-WAR PERIOD 1945-50

Political Survey of the Years 1945-50

In order to understand the problems raised by atomic weapons we must first make a survey of the political situation during the post-war period.

The cessation of hostilities and the ratification of the constitution of the United Nations at San Francisco did not mark the beginning of the peaceful era hoped for. On the contrary, the years immediately following the war were characterized by a series of measures, first by the Russians, that caused considerable anxiety: the political Russian advance into the Baltic States, in spite of the promise of independence for 'liberated states' made at the Yalta Conference, Russian pressure on Persia, who complained to the Security Council, Russian demands on Turkey for bases on the Dardanelles, the rising and the long 'civil war' in Greece from the year 1946; further the remarkable atomic bomb tests made by America at Bikini in July 1946, and the appearance of the Truman Doctrine for the protection of threatened countries—primarily Greece and Turkey—in 1947. In the same year Great Britain withdrew from India, while the policy of the USA became more flexible, with a view to preventing the Soviet Union from making new conquests (the policy of containment). The Soviet Union took steps to bind her satellites closer to her, and showed signs of wishing to make Eastern Germany communist. The so-called cold war began with the failure of the foreign minister conference in Moscow to

THE POST-WAR PERIOD 1945-50

agree on the terms of a peace treaty for Germany. America began the Marshall Plan for economic help; the Soviet Union retaliated with the Cominform organization to counteract the Marshall Plan, and made a series of mutual assistance pacts with her satellites. In the Mediterranean, where the USA had stationed large naval forces, Marshal Tito's Yugoslavia broke with Russia in June 1947.

In February 1948, the Soviet Union made a *coup d'état* in Czechoslovakia, where a communist government was established; in March, Great Britain, France, Holland, Belgium and Luxemburg signed the Brussels Treaty for mutual aid. The Soviet Union closed the highway and canal to Berlin in May, and the Western Powers met this blockade with the famous air bridge, in spite of the risk of military complications. By this time the USA had clearly taken the lead in opposing Russia, and a North Atlantic Treaty began to take form. This pact was ratified by the twelve original signatory powers on April 4, 1949. In the autumn of the same year, Western Germany began, with the approval of the Western Powers, to act as an independent state, and Russia retaliated by proclaiming Eastern Germany a sovereign state. The Russian blockade of Berlin was lifted in May 1949, after it had proved impossible to cut off Berlin and so create chaos there. In the spring of 1950, the Soviet Union and the UN came into conflict with each other on account of the Soviet demand that China should be represented by the People's Republic.

This Russian blockade of the UN was taken advantage of by the other powers when, from June 1950, outbreak of war in Korea was imminent. On June 27, President Truman announced that the USA would send military forces to Korea. In the absence of Russia no Soviet veto was forthcoming, and a large number of countries sent increasing forces to Korea to fight under American command. The USA urged the other members of NATO to increase their armaments. South Korea was liberated, but General MacArthur advanced into North Korea in November, which led to Chinese intervention and a set-back for the USA. Meanwhile the North Atlantic Treaty Organization had accepted the Pleven Plan for the creation of a European Army (abbreviated to EDC proposal). The situation was extremely unstable during the years 1950-51, and the risk of war seems to have been greatest then.

It is obvious that such conditions were very unfavourable for discussions of the reduction of tension and armaments. It is open to question whether the policy pursued by the General Assembly of the United Nations, of trying year after year to compel commissions to hold meetings at which mutual hostility was made public, was a wise one. This policy has not, at any rate, increased the prestige of the UN, but the leaders of those days considered that such meetings—with regard to world opinion and that in their own countries—were necessary under any circumstances. But to discuss a reduction of tension, while every country was straining itself to the utmost, created a special conference mentality!

Conference Problems 1946-48

It was in this post-war atmosphere that the General Assembly met in January 1946 for the first time to discuss atomic weapons. The Security Council, too, dealt with the problem raised by the Hiroshima Bomb in 1945 (6). Thus the problem of atomic weapons was approached almost a year before the question of conventional military armaments was raised. In January 1946 an international Atomic Energy Commission—AEC—consisting mainly of scientists, was appointed, and presented three reports to the Security Council during the subsequent year.

The first report, published in December 1946 (7), deals with the scientific and technical aspects of the question of the control of atomic energy, as the problem appeared to the twelve delegates at Lake Success in New York. The main question was the feasibility of an effective control, and if so, the methods to be applied. It was found practical to delegate the work to four subcommittees, which will be dealt with below. It was unanimously decided that the work should be carried out in stages, and that measures should be proceeded with step by step so that mistrust in the world should be reduced. Before starting on the second stage, the situation should have improved so much that a new step forward could really be taken. This wise principle was forgotten later on, however, which caused much trouble, and even increased political tension.

After eight weeks' hard work, the scientific-technical subcommittee was almost unanimous in its opinion that it was technically possible to organize satisfactory control, but whether it was politically possible was another question (8). Even then the difficulties arising from the fact that the uses of atomic material for peaceful or military ends were so closely connected with each other as to be 'practically inseparable' were clearly seen. These difficulties still exist, and in addition the whole atomic question has swelled out to proportions undreamt of in 1946. From a historical point of view it must be borne in mind that all that scientists knew about atomic weapons was chiefly based upon two documents which were submitted to AEC by the American delegate, that is, the American Smyth Report (9), and the more official American report called the Lilienthal Report after D. E. Lilienthal, the chairman of the American committee (10). In addition, there were certain less important American newspaper articles and the like.

International scientists established that chain reactions which released atomic energy could be obtained with three kinds of material: Uranium 235, Plutonium 239 (obtained from U 238) and Uranium 233. In any case, the raw material was uranium or thorium, and the deposits of these elements could be controlled at the mines all over the world. At that time, uranium was obtained from mines in Canada, the Belgian Congo, Czechoslovakia, and the western parts of the USA, but since 1946 enormous deposits have been discovered in many different countries. Thorium was first obtained in India, Brazil, the Dutch East Indies, Australia and other countries. The subcommittee reported that these materials could be 'fused' under control in a reactor and put to peaceful uses, or they could be made to fuse with a very rapid explosion in an atomic bomb, which is a special type of reactor. The supervision of a large number of factories was considered more difficult to realize than that of a small number. Everyone was agreed that control of all atomic weapons would have to begin with a strict supervision of mines and other sources of raw materials. The subcommittee which dealt with the legal, economic and social aspects of the problem was also unable to arrive at any precise methods of control (11).

The western world's mistrust of the Soviet Union was very great, even in 1946, when the espionage affair in Canada aroused such strong feelings, and it is historically quite natural that the USA could not accept the demands made by Russia that all atomic weapons should be prohibited, unless effective methods of control were adapted at the same time. The breaking of the Yalta Treaty by Russia was not calculated to inspire the Western Powers with confidence in the Soviet Union. This fundamental antagonism dominates the problem even today.

After the renewed transactions in 1947, in which several politicians took part, the AEC submitted a report of the results of seven months' work (March-December), full of proposals and memoranda (12). America had come to the conclusion, on the basis of meetings held during 1946, that control of the mines required right of ownership, and from that was developed the plan named after the delegate appointed by the USA, B. M. Baruch (13). All the deposits of fissionable material and all factories using such material should be owned by an international syndicate which could organize effective supervision under the aegis of the United Nations. But the Soviet Union, which had no atomic bomb at that time, insisted strongly upon a total prohibition of atomic weapons, and rejected the Baruch Plan with the question: 'With whose money will this syndicate be financed?' The Baruch Plan received a large majority in the AEC, where the Soviet Union and Poland refrained from voting. As formerly, the USA rejected any kind of atomic weapon prohibition without effective control, and the question as to whether a veto in the Security Council could prevent punitive measures against those who broke a treaty also caused great difficulties. The second session of the AEC also closed in a deadlock.

Much time was wasted by sending questions from one subcommittee to another and so on, but one valuable point was that the tasks of a control organization were set forth in detail: independent research, supervision of mines and the treatment of the raw material, the control of the distribution and stocking of material, supervision of the use of reactors, the control of the separation of isotopes in special factories, and the extent of the rights of inspection. In addition, there was the organization of the central controlling body itself, collaboration with other international and national institutions, the extraterritorial status of the personnel, which decisions should be subject to right of appeal and which were irrevocable, the penalties for the violation of treaties or others' rights, and political and other sanctions against a state that does not honour its agreements.

It is easy to see that there are an enormous number of problems, and they will probably require a very large control organization. Some scientists stated that a single mine would require about 100 supervisors if control were to be effective. What a fantastic number would be required if mines, transport, stocks and reactors were to be placed under permanent supervision! The committee's investigation has shown fully the enormous extent of the problem, if an effective, maximum control is intended. This does not detract from the value of the report of the second session if an attempt should really be made to solve the problem of control (14).

While the unrest in the Middle East and the eastern Mediterranean became more acute, and the USA applied the Truman Doctrine to give protection to threatened countries, the third session of the AEC was opened in September 1947. It is not surprising that this meeting, which went on till May 1948, was also without result, for, on November 6, 1947, Molotov declared that Russia had solved the problems attached to the construction of the atomic bomb, while in the USA it had been calculated that the Soviet Union would not get so far before 1951-52. What Molotov was then referring to was in all probability a kind of atomic bomb that the Soviet Union had constructed and which is dealt with in greater detail in Chapter 5 below. And in order to demonstrate her power, and her confidence in her own strength, the USSR took over the

THE POST-WAR PERIOD 1945-50

leadership of Czechoslovakia in May 1948 by help of Russian armed forces. In such circumstances the third session was also doomed to be without result. The majority were in favour of a proposition from the Western Powers, and Russia put forward a detailed counter proposal. The so-called Third Report of May 17, 1948, drew attention to the fact that political decisions would have to be made by the Great Powers if any results were to be achieved at all (15). The General Assembly and the Security Council were also at a dead end (16). Certain powers tried to find a solution by proposing two conventions, one with regard to the prohibition of atomic weapons and the other referring to the control of atomic weapons. Both conventions were to be put into force simultaneously. The idea was certainly sound, but could not be realized.

The AEC met again in February 1949 to test this solution, but found it impracticable, and in December the same year work was ceased. The Western Powers came to the conclusion that further transactions within the AEC seemed without prospects, a situation that was made use of by Russian propaganda, which stated that the Western Powers did not wish to come to any result, and that responsibility for the failure lay with the USA (17). At the end of 1949 Chiang Kai-shek was driven to Formosa.

Conference Problems and Certain Scientific Problems 1949-50

The consequence of this was that the work of the AEC was broken off for more than a year, while the Soviet Union in Aug.–Sept. carried out her first official atomic bomb explosion and somewhat later (at the end of 1950) solved the problem of dropping the bomb from the air. *The political significance was that during the days of the blockade* of Berlin (*spring 1948—spring 1949*) *the* USA *had a very considerable advantage over Russia as far as the atomic bomb was concerned*. Now that this is known for certain it is easier to understand how the Western Powers dared approach to the very verge of war, as was the case when the air bridge to Berlin was organized. It was only in April that the North Atlantic Treaty was signed.

Later, that is to say, at the beginning of 1950, new scientific discoveries further strengthened America's position.

In both the Western world and in Russia experiments with a new hydrogen bomb had been commenced. The fundamental principles of the hydrogen bomb are different from those of the atomic bomb. Instead of a fission of the uranium nucleus, a fusion of the hydrogen isotopes, deuterium and tritium, takes place, and helium is formed. According to Einstein's theory, loss in the mass releases far more energy than an 'ordinary' explosion. Already in 1944, three atomic scientists, Oppenheimer, Teller and Bethe, patented a hydrogen bomb which made use of a heavy hydrogen isotope, deuterium, together with an ordinary atomic bomb as detonator. It was not until long afterwards that any such bombs were made.

Preliminary work on the hydrogen bomb had shown that a so-called mass 3 hydrogen isotope, tritium, the production of which was very expensive and might take up to five years, was required ('Oppenheimer Transcripts', American State Papers, November 1954). The production of atomic bombs was therefore given priority until Russia exploded her first atomic bomb, and Klaus Fuchs, who had taken part in the discussions of the hydrogen bomb in January 1951, confessed to espionage for the Soviet Union. An extremely costly factory for the production of tritium was then established.

THE POST-WAR PERIOD 1945-50

This was the position until Dr E. Teller in 1951 invented a short cut by way of a cheaper chemical substance (probably lithium and deuterium), which was to change the situation entirely. But at the end of 1950 the USA had not yet reached the goal, although it was apparent that the solution was near. In the meantime, more practical reactors had been evolved, in which atomic energy could be released in the service of both peace and war. The atomic bomb and the hydrogen bomb increased rapidly in effect (their destructive power at the beginning of 1955 will be dealt with in Chapter 6 below) during the years 1951-55. Unlike the atomic bomb, there is no limit to the size of hydrogen bombs.

While this scientific development was taking place in deepest secrecy, discussions were still carried on in the UN. There was a feeling that the AEC, which led a precarious life, should be made part of the commission for conventional armaments which had been sitting since 1947, and which had been running idle on account of the international situation. The question was raised in the autumn of 1950 by a committee consisting of twelve members, but the war in Korea in June, and the Chinese intervention in November the same year prevented all progress. In spite of pressure brought to bear from several quarters, the USA decided, happily, not to use atomic weapons in the Korean war, from which was evolved the principle that such weapons should not be used in what the Americans called a 'border skirmish'. But it was a skirmish that cost the USA enormous losses in men and money.

At the end of the period 1945-50 the world had reached a point where rearmament made every thought of a reduction in the tension impossible, where both sides had atomic bombs, although the USA had certainly twenty times as many as Russia, and where the USA had the hydrogen bomb within reach. In Russia—in spite of Stalin's and Beria's efforts—the question of the hydrogen bomb was at a dead end, probably on account of the difficulty of obtaining tritium, but at the moment of writing the reason is not yet known for certain.

In face of the growing extent of atomic warfare, scientists had begun asking whither things were leading, and there were even politicians who began questioning the expediency of this development. And it must be said that the humanitarian and moral reaction of leading statesmen against the increase of atomic weapons was moderated by their opinion of what the interests of their own countries demanded.

Discussion of atomic problems was facilitated by a dictionary of atomic terms in five languages, compiled by the UN (18). Unesco, too, contributed with works on collective security and questions of atomic weapons (19).

Chapter 3

THE HYDROGEN BOMB PERIOD
1951-55

The Political Situation 1951. No Conferences

Characteristic for the beginning of 1951 was an enormous increase in armaments due to the Korean war. The USA quadrupled her military budget and on an average the other members of NATO doubled theirs. Steps were taken to try to prevent the export of arms and other goods of military importance to North Korea and the People's Republic of China.

General Eisenhower, the European Commander-in-Chief, had great authority, and he urged forward negotiations for a European Army, during which the attitude of Western Germany and France caused anxiety. The decree of occupation was revised and Western Germany was allowed an independent foreign office. But intense propaganda was made inside Germany, not least by the USSR, and the prospects of the EDC proposal seemed uncertain.

In March 1951, however, South Korea was free and the UN decided to be content with that. A unified command for Europe under General Eisenhower was established in April of the same year. Eisenhower considered the situation to be dangerous and demanded greater efforts from the Atlantic Powers.

Meanwhile Great Britain had suffered a serious loss of prestige by being compelled to withdraw from Abadan during the oil conflict in Persia in 1951, and in China the Communist Government was stabilized. And in September 1951 NATO was augmented by Greece and Turkey. Turkey's contribution is expected to be of considerable military importance.

In 1951 there was an intense struggle behind the scenes between East and West as to who should be first with the hydrogen bomb (20), and to prepare the propaganda to be linked up with it. In the middle of the year, the USA had begun to make certain preliminary tests with the bomb.

The Soviet Union had prepared a propaganda offensive for 1951, which, by stressing the idea of peace, was to place the USA in an unfavourable light. The communist-inspired 'World Council for Peace' met in Stockholm on March 3-4, 1951, and the 'peace parliament' proposed that the great powers, including the People's Republic of China, should conclude a peace treaty. The fact that this is to be found in the first paragraph of the United Nations constitution did not worry them at all. The Stockholm Appeal, which was by no means a credit to Sweden's capital, was used all over the world to further the interests of the USSR. The resolution maintained that the government first using the atomic bomb against any other country would by so doing commit a crime against humanity. As Ö. Undén, the Swedish Foreign Minister, said, it would have been more important to pronounce that any country beginning a war of aggression, with or without atomic weapons, would be committing a crime against humanity (21). But the object of the initiators was not to brand every aggressor, but to make the USA appear as the greatest threat to peace, and at the same time strike a blow for the recognition of Communist China. The World Council for Peace announced later that all the people in the Middle

THE HYDROGEN BOMB PERIOD 1951-54

East and North Africa should be freed from oppression and intervention from without, but omitted to demand that the Soviet Union's satellite states should be granted the same privileges!

Fear of the atomic bomb and of the danger of the coming hydrogen bomb were, therefore, used one-sidedly for a single political purpose.

No conferences of any importance to the atomic weapon question were held that year, but Dr Teller's discovery, mentioned above, saw the light of day, and certain tests with the hydrogen bomb were made in the USA in the spring and summer of 1951.

The Political Situation 1952

There was a short crisis in NATO after 1951, due to the fact that the USA at the Lisbon Conference in February 1952 carried through a decision that during 1952-54 armaments should be considerably increased, against which several member states reacted. America's demands were greatly reduced in December 1952. The Soviet Union made certain proposals with regard to the German question: an all-Germany government, the withdrawal of troops from Germany, etc., while the Western Powers signed a peace treaty with Western Germany, which state was to be included in the proposed EDC.

The Russian leaders struck more conciliatory tones now and again during 1952, but at the same time they took steps to remove from the satellite states all people not faithful to Moscow. Within the Western Powers there was a tug-of-war for the EDC organization during the years 1951 and 1952. In May of the latter year an EDC pact was signed, only to be annulled later.

Conference Problems 1952

In spite of the Korean war, the General Assembly of the United Nations, which met first in Paris and later in New York, had, during the winter 1951-52, taken up the question of disarmament, and avoided discussion of Korea (22). The committee of twelve, appointed in 1950 to deal with the proposed amalgamation of the AEC and the commission for conventional arms, decided that a new Disarmament Commission (DC) should be convened to deal with both problems. The Western Powers proposed a balanced reduction of armaments, while the Soviet Union wanted membership of NATO and the holding of military bases in foreign countries to disqualify for membership in the United Nations, and put forward the proposal for peace made by the World Council for Peace. As a result, only the united DC came into being in January 1952, after local armistice negotiations were begun in Korea and the outlook there had become more hopeful. The new DC was given very extensive tasks which proved sufficient to last until both sides had the hydrogen bomb! It was soon found that the discussion of atomic weapons was drowned in the flood of problems which conventional armaments alone occasioned. At the same time previous experience was confirmed: positive results could hardly be expected in such questions before a decrease in political tension made possible a reduction of armaments.

The DC sat from February 4 till the end of the year. Some details may be found in the present writer's articles in February and March, 1953 (23), the Commission's minutes (24) and the final report mentioned below. The DC still consisted of representatives of the governments sitting in the Security Council, and Canada. On the whole the Western Powers advocated a balanced reduction on the

THE HYDROGEN BOMB PERIOD 1951-54

grounds that the risk of war would be reduced by equality in arms. The question was raised as to whether atomic weapons and conventional armaments could be combined so that ten large atomic bombs would equal, for instance, a certain number of army divisions, and reductions be made on this basis. An attempt was made to fix a 'ceiling' for the military manpower of the great powers and thus achieve equilibrium between the Western Powers and the USSR and China.

The Western Powers were willing to prohibit the use of atomic weapons, but only if the Soviet Union would agree to effective control. But Russia considered that the Baruch Plan would lead to an 'over-trust' of which the USA would become the leader. During the autumn session of the Commission in 1952, a French compromise proposal was discussed: a first stage with the verification of existing conventional armaments, a second when a reduction of such armaments was made and atomic weapons were prohibited, and a third with further reductions and the destruction of atomic weapons. The Western Powers agreed that the prohibition of the use of atomic weapons should begin already in the first stage, but the USSR demanded that the manufacture of atomic weapons should also cease at the beginning of this stage. The final report of the DC on October 9, 1952, received eleven votes against the Soviet Union's one.

In 1952 the General Council debated the reports of the commissions, and the USA maintained that all states should deliver exact information on both kinds of armaments. This was, from the point of view of the USA, a departure from the principle that the production of atomic weapons should, to large extent, be kept secret. But the USA demanded control by means of strict inspection. Russia proposed the settlement of the Korean war, the withdrawal of troops from Korea, a reduction of armaments, the prohibition of atomic weapons, and a certain degree of control.

The USA exploded her first hydrogen bomb in November 1952, and in August 1953 the Soviet Union achieved the same result. (It was not, however, until March 1954 that the USA dropped her first hydrogen bomb from an aeroplane. This time Russia was first.) The situation at the end of 1952, as far as atomic weapons were concerned, was that the USA was ahead with the hydrogen bomb, while its stock of atomic bombs, which was probably ten times as great as that of Russia, gave security from a Russian war of aggression. It was in 1952 that both sides increased their interest in the smaller, so-called tactical atomic weapons, and the USA began to convert some existing atomic bombs into hydrogen bombs.

The Political Situation 1953

President Truman, in his message in January 1953, said that humanity had now crossed the threshold of a new era, and that human beings were able to lay waste a civilization that had been built up with great sacrifices during hundreds of generations. At the same time, the Churchill government made a revaluation of Russia's intentions. It was assumed that the cold war would continue, but that the superiority of the Allies with regard to atomic bombs made war unlikely in the immediate future. The meeting of the Atlantic Council at the end of 1952 influenced the situation by deciding that the activities of the Atlantic Powers should be global. Equilibrium in armaments, which might form a fair basis for a reduction in armaments as soon as tension in the world diminished, had been arrived at in the beginning of 1953. America's

THE HYDROGEN BOMB PERIOD 1951-54

tactical atomic weapons, as was publicly stressed by General Ridgway, who had succeeded Eisenhower on the latter's election as President, contributed largely to this equilibrium.

Stalin's death on March 5, 1953, aroused general curiosity as to how the 'new Russian regime' would behave. An analysis of this has been made by the present writer (26).

The leaders of the USA were of the opinion that, independent of eventual possibilities of improvements in the situation, it was necessary to continue with the development of the hydrogen bomb, and in proof of this a number of hydrogen bomb tests were made in the Pacific from March to May (see Chapter 4).

From the political point of view it should be observed that the armistice in Korea came into force on June 27 that year, but the problem of the prisoners of war was long unsolved.

The situation in Europe was as follows: the Soviet Union crushed the disturbances that had been taking place in Eastern Germany ever since June 1953, continued her policy of russification in the whole of eastern Europe, and did all she could to prevent the organization of a European Army, which organization was supported by the majority of the Western Powers. The latter were in favour of an open alliance with Western Germany, advocated that state's rearmament, and the formation of a European Army with the support of France, Western Germany, Italy, Holland, Belgium and Luxemburg, while Great Britain remained aloof for the time being. Russia's plan for the neutralization of Germany was rejected by the Western Powers, but, as will be shown later, it resulted in certain limitations in the military strength and atomic weapons of Western Germany.

INTERNATIONAL ATOMIC POLICY

An armistice came into force in Korea on June 27, 1953, but no peace treaties were forthcoming for Germany and Japan. The Western Powers agreed, at the Bermuda Conference in December 1953, on concerted action in certain questions.

When the first Russian H-bomb had been tested in August, President Eisenhower announced that the USSR was in a position to carry out an air attack on the USA, by which many understood an attack with hydrogen bombs. The political conference to deal with peace in Korea was slow in opening, and the war in Indo-China increased in extent. The double threat of the hydrogen bomb was now a possibility to be reckoned with.

Conference Problems 1953

The idea of attempting to reduce the state of tension by stages (27) began to gain ground, as did the opinion that the American system of 'maximum control' was no longer practicable and that there was good reason to investigate different forms of 'minimum control'. By this is meant the minimum control necessary for the more or less extensive limitations in the use of atomic weapons, the prohibition of the manufacture of certain kinds of such weapons, and an agreement regarding the destruction of the types of weapons prohibited.

The report issued by the 1952 DC was discussed in the General Assembly in March 1953. The majority proposal that the DC should continue its work was again on the agenda. The American representative asked the Russian if, now that Stalin was dead, there was any chance of a more constructive discussion, but the Russian delegate answered evasively that the delay was due wholly to the fact that the USA refused to accept an unconditional pro-

THE HYDROGEN BOMB PERIOD 1951-54

hibition of atomic weapons. The general feeling within the DC was that a more favourable political situation was necessary. At the meeting of the General Assembly from August to November 1953, the British delegate asserted that anyone proposing a great reduction of atomic weapons without control did not really take the problem seriously, while the French delegate was in favour of a compromise whereby the problem would be solved in three stages (28). On December 8, 1953, President Eisenhower addressed the General Assembly and proposed an atom 'bank', which will be dealt with in Chapter 4 below.

The Political Situation 1954-55

The conference of foreign ministers in Berlin caused great pessimism when it was realized that the USSR among other things did not intend to make any concessions regarding Austria and Germany. But it was agreed to continue discussion of the atomic question, which has been carried on chiefly through diplomatic channels between the USA and Russia (UN Documents A/2738/54).

President Eisenhower said in June that a wise foreign policy must aim at 'building up a force that can frustrate any foolhardy communist aggression', and 'Major Problems of United States Foreign Policy', 1954 (29), emphasized that the aim of American foreign policy is still to acquire the greatest possible state, military and economic power to oppose Soviet communism. The commander-in-chief of the NATO forces, General Gruenther, reported that military equilibrium had been attained, as a consequence of which the risk of war had diminished somewhat. An armistice was signed by Viet-Nam, Laos and Cambodia on July 21.

Great Britain supported the American atomic policy,

and Churchill declared that only America's lead in atomic and hydrogen bombs prevented Europe's complete subjugation under communist tyranny.

The Soviet Union won a political success at the end of August when the EDC proposal was defeated in the French National Assembly, but the situation was changed later by the London-Paris agreement, which will be dealt with in Chapter 4 below. Great Britain's promise to take part in the defence of Europe made possible great progress in the uniting of Europe. The Western Powers refused to negotiate with the Soviet Union until their parliaments had ratified the agreements.

At the end of the year Russia proposed the withdrawal of troops from both Eastern and Western Germany, and also proposed consultation on the size of the police forces. At the same time the Russians threatened to form an Eastern European Military Alliance, to be realized by the new regime in the USSR, which assumed power in February 1955. Collaboration between Russia and the People's Republic of China was extended to a certain degree.

Conference Problems 1954-55

In face of this world-wide situation, the conferences dealing with atomic problems and armaments developed hesitatingly. The UN Disarmament Commission decided to continue its work in London during the summer of 1954 as a smaller subcommittee, and secret meetings were held to prevent conference propaganda. From a summary published recently by the present author (30) may be quoted some words. It was established at the secret meetings—the minutes were published later—that certain advances had been made in several spheres, but that differences of opinion in politically important questions still existed.

THE HYDROGEN BOMB PERIOD 1951-54

After the situation had improved somewhat by the cessation of hostilities in Indo-China, the DC took up the subcommittee's report in New York in July 1954. The question of control was, as usual, the great stumbling-block. A compromise was proposed by France and Great Britain, but it was denounced by the Soviet Union who would not relinquish the demand that an unconditional prohibition of atomic weapons should precede a reduction of conventional armaments, but agreed that the work should be planned in two stages. The 'basis' created then was as follows: atomic weapons were only to be used as a defence against aggression; it was agreed to reduce conventional armaments and create a control system for atomic weapons and afterwards stop the manufacture of such weapons and proceed with their destruction after conventional armaments had been considerably reduced. But Russia wanted the prohibition of the use of atomic weapons to be unconditional, and accepted only a small proportion of the control proposed by the Western Powers. No unanimity was reached, and the position in the autumn DC was on the whole unchanged.

At the meeting of the General Assembly in September, Russia astonished the world by accepting the French-British plan as a basis for further negotiations. This was at the time when the EDC proposal had failed, and the Soviet Union deemed it unwise to unite the Western Powers too closely. Russia proposed (UN Document A/2742/54) that the DC should prepare a convention based on a decrease of tension in two stages according to the following timetable: the first stage was to consist of a reduction of conventional armaments and military budgets, and at the same time an international control commission to supervise ordinary disarmament should be set up under the Security Council. The second stage was to consist partly of a further reduction of conventional weapons, partly complete prohibition of atomic, biological and chemical weapons, now known as 'ABC weapons', and the cessation of manufacture and the destruction of such weapons. Thus atomic weapons would disappear at the beginning of the second stage. But up to now the Soviet has retained the right of veto within the Security Council, and no agreement has been reached with regard to the powers of the control organization.

The General Assembly also decided that new efforts should be made, that the subcommittee of the DC should try to reach a solution, and the DC should report to the Security Council and the General Assembly. In the course of the discussions in the Assembly, Sweden's representative, R. Sandler, stressed that a result must be arrived at with regard to the method of control, and emphasized that the question of atomic weapons must not be put off, for if nothing was done to solve this problem, no result would be forthcoming in the question of disarmament. This is without doubt the heart of the matter.

The last phase of the work of the United Nations during the year 1954 was the meeting of the General Assembly in November, when, after diverse discussions in the political committee and the Assembly, it was decided to submit a plan to serve as a working programme for the subcommittee (UN Documents A, Resolution 216, November 5, 1954). According to this plan, efforts should be made to achieve both a general reduction of armaments and prohibition of nuclear weapons and all kinds of arms leading to mass destruction, and arrive at effective international control. With the approval of Russia it was stated that the necessary control organization should have the right, power and function to guarantee that reductions agreed upon, of all kinds of weapons and armed forces, as well as the prohibition of nuclear and other weapons for mass destruction, are honoured, and to ensure the use of atomic energy only in the interests of peace. It is the task of the subcommittee of the DC to find an acceptable solution at a time when the race for armaments, and particular for nuclear weapons, is increasing.

President Eisenhower's atom bank proposal and the decision of the General Assembly on November 6, 1954, will lead to an international technical conference on worldwide collaboration in the application of atomic energy to the cause of peace. This Conference started in August 1955.

When it was discovered that fissionable material could be denatured, which makes it useless for atomic bombs, a method was found to make possible the realization of the atom bank. Denatured material can be rendered suitable for atomic bombs only by a long, expensive process, but this problem has not yet been finally solved.

The general secretary of the United Nations, D. Hammarskjöld, formed a special atomic bureau at the end of the year, with the view of intensifying the work.

The close of 1954 was completely dominated by the energetic efforts of Russia to overthrow the Western European Union. Russian pressure was particularly brought to bear upon France, and the Franco-Russian Treaty of 1944 was used to create opposition to the Union in France, and German opposition was encouraged by the announcement that the Union would make the reunion of Eastern and Western Germany impossible for all time.

The political intrigues culminated in a very tense period at the turn of the year, when the French parliament approved the rearmament of Western Germany, but this very important measure was by no means concluded at the beginning of 1955.

A few circumstances closely connected with the problem of nuclear weapons and the extremely interesting diplomatic discussions in December 1954 of the use of nuclear weapons by NATO powers are dealt with in the last part of Chapter 4.

The United Nations DC sat in London till June, and is to meet later in New York. The negotiations were of a private nature, but on May 11 Russia made certain proposals which complied with part of the wishes of the Western Powers. The final result is uncertain at the time of writing (May 1955), but negotiations will be continued in New York during the summer.

The Norwegian Nobel Institute in Oslo is to organize, with help from the USA, a meeting of delegates from thirteen countries (not including the Eastern Powers), at which among other questions the possibility of a reduction in the political tension will be dealt with.

In the spring of 1955, the information department of the UN sent out a printed summary of the discussions held in recent years. It is to be hoped that the title, 'A Step Forward', will hold true of the year 1955.

Chapter 4

THE WESTERN POWERS' VIEW OF THE PROBLEMS

There are so many valuable sources available for those who wish to study the atomic policy of the Western Powers during the past decade, that it is extremely difficult to make a choice. Only the facts and printed sources which may be considered to have influenced development considerably are touched upon in the present work, in which conditions in the USA are predominant.

USA

The USA 1945-50

B. M. Baruch, the American representative to the international AEC, presented, in connection with the Smyth and Lilienthal reports mentioned above, further scientific information (31). The USA's own national atomic energy commission also submitted a report on the possibility of controlling atomic energy, and recommended an atomic policy based on placing all the sources of fissionable material under an international syndicate, which was the only way to achieve effective control (32). The *Bulletin of Atomic Scientists*, published in Chicago, soon became a leading international periodical in the field of atomic science.

'The Carnegie Endowment for International Peace' took up the whole question for general discussion (33), set people to work to find out where fissionable material was to be found in the world, and searched for scientists—who spoke in favour of a general moratorium with regard to the manufacture of atomic weapons. The policy favoured by the American government was, however, to obtain a margin of security against the Soviet by laying up a stock of atomic weapons, a security deemed very necessary since developments in the Balkans and Germany had caused a long period of anxiety. A. W. Dulles (34) asserted in 1947 that a reduction of atomic weapons ought to take place through the medium of the United Nations at the same time as a general reduction of armaments, which later became the official policy of the USA.

At the same time public opinion was greatly influenced by a book entitled 'One World or None', written jointly by a number of America's leading atomic experts and published in the USA. This work stressed the danger of the situation, and urged that energetic efforts should be made towards the establishment of some kind of world government (35). A discussion also flared up in the USA as to whether it had been necessary in the last stages of the war to use the atomic bomb against Japan. J. F. Byrnes in his book, 'Speaking Frankly' (1947), pointed out the reasons which led to that decision. Somewhat later H. W. Baldwin, the military writer, and E. M. Zacharias, one of the heads of the naval information department, raised the objection that the use of the bomb against Japan was not worth the price, and that Japan was ready to capitulate even before the bomb was dropped (36). K. T. Compton, on the other hand, in an earlier work entitled 'If the Bomb had not been used', maintained that failure to drop the bomb would have meant many more months of bloodshed and destruction in the war in Asia. This led President Truman to declare officially that it was he who personally decided that the atomic bombs should be used against Japan, and that in this he had the support of his advisers.

THE WESTERN POWERS' VIEW OF THE PROBLEMS

The war-time collaboration between Great Britain and the USA was broken off in 1946, when it was discovered that atomic secrets had leaked out to the Soviet. Much legislation now grew up round the atomic industries: an Atomic Energy Act was passed in 1946, supervision regulations for mines, production and security, economic rules, directions touching on radioactive materials, the reorganization of the atomic energy commission and so on, all saw the light of day. The atomic energy commission delivered half-yearly reports to Congress, some of which were published and discussed publicly. These reports are of immense value.

All activities dealing with atomic problems were covered by a number of protective measures, often called the 'atomic curtain'. But there were many scientists, and more particularly journalists, who took care that the American public knew far more about what was happening than, for instance, did the people of Russia. Even so a large amount of special literature on the utilization of the atom to create fuel, electricity, new medicine, radiological by-products, protection from radioactive rays and new materials in the service of agriculture, had appeared in the USA before 1948.

With regard to atomic weapons, the tests made at Bikini (37) in 1946 should be borne in mind. These tests were called 'Operation Crossroads' in the USA, a name that indicated that America was in some doubt as to what atomic policy would be wisest in the future. From the results of the tests the USA came to the conclusion that it was essential to extend the atomic industry considerably and at the same time spread out the plants over large areas in relatively sparsely populated districts, and that ships should be protected by special measures.

When atomic bomb tests, 'Operation Sandstone', were

made in 1948, a bomb six times as powerful as that dropped on Hiroshima was exploded.

In 'The Price of Power', the well-known book by H. W. Baldwin (38), it was emphasized that the USA could be the target for atomic bomb attacks in the future, and that America's front was along the Baltic and the Adriatic. The possibility of an immense threat was the only thing that could subdue Russia's craving for expansion. American opinion was shocked by the affair of Alger Hiss in 1949 and the so-called Kosenkina episode, which led to the closing of several consulates both in the Soviet and the USA, and the cold war became even chillier during the years 1948-49.

The Russian blockade of Berlin in the spring of 1948 and the ratification of the North Atlantic Treaty in March-July 1949 were important contributory causes. In the former case the Western Powers retaliated with the famous air bridge, an action which would perhaps hardly have been risked had not the Allies been in possession of the atomic bomb.

It was, therefore, a shock for the USA when the Soviet in Aug.–Sept. 1949 exploded her first atomic bomb, called in America 'Joe one'. Then the federative German republic was formed, to which the Soviet retaliated by creating an Eastern German republic. President Truman gave a speech (39) in which he said that it had always been expected that the secrets of the atomic bomb would be laid bare in other countries, but events had greatly emphasized the need for international control of atomic energy. In January 1950, President Truman declared that he had given the American atomic energy commission instructions to produce a hydrogen bomb, and that until a satisfactory method of control had been found, the USA would continue to take the lead (40). But no large bomb tests were made in the USA during 1949 and 1950.

Great interest was also aroused by statements made by B. M. Baruch, Mumford, Richardson and others in an article entitled 'Atom Bomb', which dealt with the problem from different angles (41), taking into consideration the expected hydrogen bomb, whose greater power of destruction brought many problems to a climax. At the same time, the Federation of American Scientists appealed to President Truman for a new and more flexible atomic policy in America.

The so-called Stockholm Appeal for Peace, 1950, was used assiduously in the USA by all those who feared that the world was heading for a catastrophe, and the publishers of the *Bulletin of Atomic Scientists* gave a summary of the situation (42). Einstein took part in the violent discussion too (43), and 1950 was rightly considered a 'Year of Decision'. It was in such a situation that the Korean war broke out on June 25, 1950.

The reports of the American atomic energy commission during the years 1949-50 were influenced by the situation, and opinions were divided for and against the hydrogen bomb. Gordon Dean and Admiral Lewis Strauss worked for the hydrogen bomb, and Dean Acheson, the Secretary of State, and L. Johnson, the Secretary of Defence, were also in favour. The problem of civil defence and attacks by atomic weapons was the subject of much investigation in Congress, the defence department and the atomic energy commission (44), but the practical steps advanced only slowly on account of economic and other reasons. The events of the Korean war led to an increase in efforts.

On the threshold of the hydrogen bomb era, H. A. Bethe, the atomic specialist, proposed that the USA should declare that she would not be the first power to use the hydrogen bomb, but would only fall back upon it if attacked. R. E. Lapp considered that the only possible means of defence would be to spread out the large towns as much as possible, which, of course, would have far-reaching economic consequences. Air Marshal C. A. Spaatz showed what security foreign hydrogen bomb attack would cost in terms of air defence. Prominence was also given in the press to the circumstance that the Mayor of Hiroshima, S. Hamai, then made public a new calculation of the number of victims at Hiroshima; 210,000 to 240,000 dead. The incredible amount of destruction that could be expected of a hydrogen bomb attack on large towns made the American public hold its breath for a moment. But the American leaders were of the opinion that work on the hydrogen bomb had to go on because of the risk of the Soviet's being first in the field and using the bomb as a threat of war in the hazardous situation prevailing at that time. When the political situation of those days is taken into consideration, it is easier to understand the steps taken by the American government. The danger of the Russians being the first was far too great after Klaus Fuchs was exposed as a spy in January 1950.

Feelings ran high in the USA during the Korean war. Churchmen and Quakers joined in the discussion as to whether the hydrogen bomb was 'right or wrong', and advocated an agreement between East and West. Atomic specialists such as J. R. Oppenheimer, H. A. Bethe, D. R. Inglis, G. Dean, the chairman of the atomic energy commission, Senator B. McMahon (creator of the McMahon law), A. Einstein, H. C. Urey, N. Bohr, the famous Danish nuclear physicist, and many others took part in the non-technical discussion (45).

In the meantime legislation dealing with problems of atomic energy had increased considerably and made necessary the publication of a synopsis of the regulations in force. The Senate and the House of Representatives had a joint committee, the so-called Joint Committee on Atomic Energy, to deal with all questions pertaining to atomic science. Some representatives of the government seemed to share the doubts of scientists in the face of the hydrogen bomb era, while others emphasized the dictates of power. Even nuclear physicists pointed out that America's foreign policy had been greatly influenced by the atomic and hydrogen bombs (46).

The Western powers had a greater feeling of security after a single command was established for the North Atlantic Treaty defence forces at the end of 1950.

The USA 1951-52

The hydrogen bomb (H-bomb) was nearing its completion, as shown in Chapter 2 above, and 'Operation Greenhouse' was carried out in the Marshall Islands in 1951, under the leadership of Teller and General Quesada. This bomb was fitted with cooling apparatus to keep the temperature of the tritium and deuterium at a very low level.

But it was not until November 2, 1952—just before Eisenhower's election to the presidency—that the first H-bomb was exploded at Eniwetok in the Pacific Ocean, 'Operation Ivy', with the bomb 'Mike', and after that it took another fifteen months before a hydrogen bomb that could be dropped from an aeroplane was forthcoming. The reason for this delay is still a matter of conjecture. The whole of the dramatic race against time has been described in a much quoted but very adversely criticized book by J. Shepley and Cl. Blair, entitled 'The Hydrogen Bomb' (46a). It is claimed that America's delay with the hydrogen bomb was due to political and moral apprehensions, which almost gave the Soviet the lead, and that there had been rivalry between the supporters of Teller and those of Oppenheimer, and that the former were actuated by considerations of national security and the latter by the fear that the hydrogen bomb would be a means to enable the USA to follow a still harsher foreign policy. On the other hand it has been stated in the USA that the laboratories in Los Alamos had been working on the problem for a long time without delay, and that the first project for a hydrogen bomb was very impractical. The war in Korea undermined all opposition, particularly after Teller had found a better solution.

One circumstance which seriously disturbed American opinion was the risk of radioactive contamination from the bomb tests, and the radioactive ash which might be carried long distances by capricious winds. The American atomic energy commission replied that all possible caution was observed, and the commission's new chairman, Admiral Lewis L. Strauss, declared that the tests were a domestic problem for the USA, and that they would continue until the manufacture of atomic weapons and the use of them was prohibited. 'The USA considers that a continuance of the experiments will deter the Soviet from beginning war' was the official statement. American public opinion was shocked by the Soviet's brusque dismissal of the American ambassador to Moscow, G. Kennan, in the autumn of 1952.

The years 1951-52 were years of trial for the American authorities, but in view of the fact that it was known that the Soviet was not far behind the USA with the hydrogen bomb, it must be admitted that, from a historical-political point of view, America had no other choice than to hasten the production of the hydrogen bomb. The USA considered quite rightly that it was impossible to influence public

THE WESTERN POWERS' VIEW OF THE PROBLEMS

opinion in the Soviet, and even if it were possible, there was no hope that it would make any impression on the actions of the Russian leaders.

The USA 1953

The struggle for the world's uranium deposits had now become more bitter. There was a 'uranium-rush' in the same style as the old 'gold-rush'. A large number of deposits were discovered in the USA, but they were quite inadequate. By the beginning of 1953, however, the USA had succeeded in increasing her import of uranium from the Belgian Congo, the South African Union, Australia and Canada. Canada had then a considerable production of uranium. All this required extensive commercial activity.

It was also while the Korean war was raging, that the manufacture of small, so-called tactical atomic weapons to meet the demands of the various branches of defence was begun.

No fewer than eleven atomic bomb tests were carried out at the Nevada testing grounds, during which military personnel were given a certain amount of training in protective measures. The establishments in the Marshall Islands (Bikini), at Savannah River, Oak Ridge, Los Alamos, Portsmouth and so on were extended to suit the requirements of hydrogen bomb tests. The Joint Committee on Atomic Energy, consisting of nine senators and nine members of the House of Representatives, served as a link with the authorities responsible for financial grants (47).

The work was intensified during the latter part of the year, America's atomic energy received 3.35 per cent of the total annual budget. In addition, new power stations, based on the use of fissionable material, were built. New atomic bomb tests were prepared and the hydrogen bomb laboratory at Livermore was enlarged. The machines for the atom-powered submarine, the *Nautilus*, were constructed, and an aeroplane engine was planned, but the development of civil industries was also encouraged.

The fact, stated by the American AEC, that the Soviet exploded her first hydrogen bomb on August 12, 1953, clearly without cooling apparatus, was the cause of profound self-examination in America.

Towards the end of the year, President Eisenhower proposed the establishment of a 'bank' of fissionable materials, to which every state should contribute a certain amount of material to be used solely in the interests of peace. The proposal was received with enthusiasm by the Western Powers and those in agreement with them, but was adversely criticized by the Soviet, who asserted that the USA made the proposal in order to hide the fact that America declined to agree to the total prohibition of atomic weapons. In view of the uncertainty in the world at large, and the risk of communist expansion by means of more or less warlike methods, the USA was naturally unwilling to destroy her atomic weapons. One must in fairness bear in mind that, although an armistice had been signed in Korea, the difficult question of the prisoners of war still unsolved and the war in Indo-China had assumed greater proportions. And there was good reason for the USA to feel suspicious of spies.

Senator McCarthy's efforts were crowned with success in December 1953, and the world-famous atomic physicist, J. R. Oppenheimer, considered by many as the creator of the atomic bomb, but who had perhaps been somewhat incautious in the choice of his acquaintances, was denied all access to atomic secrets. This decision was supported by the chairman of the atomic commission, Strauss. It is true that Oppenheimer, like many other scientists, had been opposed to the production of the proposed hydrogen bomb, but when Teller made his new discovery Oppenheimer worked for the realization of the project. From this it is easy to understand how high feelings could run in discussions of atomic problems. It is no exaggeration to say that America's superiority over the Soviet was for many sober-minded Americans a matter of national survival. It was only natural that events in Korea, Indo-China and other places confirmed their feelings.

The USA 1954-55

H. W. Baldwin and others showed at the beginning of 1954 (49) that international control of atomic energy must be considered of prime importance to the future of humanity. Hydrogen bombs could demolish even the largest towns, said nuclear physicists. The growing stock of atomic bombs in the Soviet would allow that country to exert more political pressure on America's allies in Western Europe and Asia. Baldwin favoured the prohibition of the use of atomic weapons but would allow their manufacture for the time being, and the retention of existing stocks. He came to the interesting conclusion that America might win a nominal victory over the Soviet by the use of atomic weapons, but she could not win a political victory. 'Atomic warfare will not lead to victory but to chaos.'

Thus there are, even in military circles, people who are sceptical with regard to the use of large atomic weapons. The Secretary of State, J. F. Dulles, made a statement in the defence debate in March 1954 to the effect that the

USA relied mainly on her ability to strike immediately wherever necessary and with whatever weapons she herself might choose. Later he stated that he by no means wished to recommend a total atomic war, but only the 'possibility' to carry on such a war. The Commander-in-Chief, Admiral Radford, looked upon atomic weapons as conventional weapons, which does not suggest that he is willing to do away with them. In May B. M. Baruch maintained that the Soviet's claim to have reduced her military budget was false, for in reality the means had only been transferred to the metallurgical and chemical industries. A press quarrel blew up, in which the Soviet denied that that was the case.

President Eisenhower has made several statements (50) which indicate, among other things, that in the first place a war in which the hydrogen bomb would be used should be avoided. General Gruenther has said that a Russian attack on Western Europe would end in defeat for Russia on account of the superiority of America in atomic weapons. H. W. Baldwin calculates that the USA has 5,000 atomic and hydrogen bombs against Russia's 500-1,000. According to Admiral Strauss, America has about as many atomic weapons as she needs, which is now called a 'state of saturation'. The USA has resolved to exchange information about atomic weapons with the members of the Atlantic Treaty.

A special minister for disarmament, Harold Stassen, who is entrusted with the task of drawing up the outlines of the atomic policy, has been appointed in the USA in 1955. In questions of armaments the difficulty remains that while the Soviet demands a proportional reduction, the Western Powers want a top limit for all military forces (for Great Britain and France 650,000 men, for the Soviet, China and the USA one to one and a half million men), and

THE WESTERN POWERS' VIEW OF THE PROBLEMS

maintain that the Soviet control plan is far too sketchy—particularly during the first period—to be accepted.

In 1954 the production of uranium increased, and there was a drop in the price. New factories were established in the USA, Britain, Canada and other countries (51). Two atom-powered submarines are now completed and a number of private firms are studying power reactors. Several testing grounds have been granted freedom from the states in which they lie—a kind of local autonomy—which has proved necessary.

Bomb tests with hydrogen bombs that could be dropped from aeroplanes have been carried out in the Pacific since March 1954 ('Operation Castle'), under the leadership of the USA atomic energy commission in the presence of representatives of all branches of defence, and thus the USA had caught up with the Soviet. Since 1945, the USA has exploded more than forty atomic bombs. During the winter 1954-55 more than fifteen tests were carried out (mostly in the Nevada Desert), including small atomic weapons of 3,000 to 8,000 tons trotyl explosive force, that is to say, much less than the power of the Hiroshima atomic bomb. The greater part of the American press, however, is not in favour of dangerous hydrogen bomb tests.

The American view of the problem of atomic weapons has been the subject of special study by the author (52), who came to the conclusion that universal disarmament in the sphere of atomic weapons is still the 'official' standpoint or hope. While military spokesmen often mention the use of atomic weapons in war, most scientists are definitely against it. The government point of view seems to be that the bomb will only be used against those who, in a 'great war', begin to use atomic weapons, by which is meant large atomic and hydrogen bombs, much more destructive than the Hiroshima bomb. This is called in the USA 'the reprisal theory'. The USA demands effective control as a condition for the abolition of atomic weapons, but the Soviet has not yet accepted that point of view. But now that both parties can injure each other incalculably, it has become more necessary for humanity to find something better than merely to rely on the threat of the bomb to avert war. It is by no means certain that a 'total war' will even lead to a victorious peace; it may create circumstances that will lead to revolutions. It is generally considered in the USA that the smaller atomic weapons are part of ordinary armaments.

Finally, a few words about the most recent legislation, the atomic factories and so on. The American atomic energy commission of 1953-54 took the initiative to a number of alterations in the Atomic Energy Act. The commission has now the right to make long term contracts with private firms, the right to increase the number of plants for defence purposes, to employ armed guards and to relieve the commission's factories from all taxes. The increased demand for personnel has made necessary several measures; new establishments for the training of nuclear physicists, and an Advisory Committee on Industrial Information attends to contacts with the public, press and industry. Experimental stations have been established at several universities. Instruction in the legislative measures for the protection of the inhabitants from injury caused by atomic factories, radioactive contamination from the clouds and so on has been greatly increased. Films are also used to give the public information about civil defence problems. Since 1954 power reactors and certain amounts of uranium may be sold to foreign countries. There are already more than thirty reactors in the USA, many of which are for purely peaceful purposes (53). The atomic energy commission has now twenty-eight

THE WESTERN POWERS' VIEW OF THE PROBLEMS

specialists in charge of various testing stations and factories. There is a tendency for the state to leave the production of energy for peaceful purposes to private or local government bodies, and to relieve the commission of these problems. Foreigners may now go through courses in the management of reactors in the USA. Since the alteration of the Atomic Energy Acts the allies of the USA are also given information about the production of atomic weapons, and how their armed forces should be trained in peacetime.

The Colorado Plateau, in the inland, south-western part of the USA, has continued to be the centre for the production of raw material. In addition there are mines in South Dakota, Wyoming, Montana, Arizona and other places, and it became necessary to open about thirty local offices of the atomic energy commission whose area covers the whole of the USA. These offices establish contacts and draw up contracts with all the private firms working in that sphere. The state had already invested 4,000,000,000 dollars at the beginning of 1953. In 1953 were added 3,500,000 dollars, and the total sum had grown considerably by 1954. New testing grounds are being opened up, and a great number of atomic towns have been established. Development is proceeding very rapidly.

There were 530 uranium mines in the USA in 1954, and new sources are being found continually on the Colorado Plateau and elsewhere. There are more than fifteen mines with an annual production of above 100,000 tons each. Canada delivers large quantities of uranium to the USA from the mines at Eldorado by the Great Bear Lake, Lake Athabaska, in Ontario, Mississagi and other places (51). Further information may be obtained from Appendices 2 and 3.

The 1954 report of the American atomic energy commission emphasizes that atomic energy will play a very important part in the supply of power in all countries without sufficient coal, liquid fuel or electricity to meet the increasing demand that the future will bring.

A Gallup poll in the USA has shown that the danger for large towns is now understood by the general public, but in spite of that only 12 per cent were contemplating moving from towns to escape the bomb threat. Sixty-nine per cent are in agreement with the government policy that no control plan can be accepted that does not include 'strict inspection'. But the meaning of 'strict inspection' has not been defined.

An international organization has been established during 1955 to deal with the purchase of atomic research materials. At present the USA, Great Britain, Canada, France, Australia, South Africa and Portugal are represented.

F. R. Dulles, in his recent book 'America's Rise to World Power', has pointed out that it has been the wish of the Soviet to maintain the right of veto which has made progress in the atomic weapons question impossible, and that the relative strength with regard to atomic weapons has played a large part in all the important decisions during the decade 1945-55.

WESTERN EUROPE

The Western European Union

The European states belonging to the Western Powers have also developed their atomic policy in harmony with their foreign policy. The original Brussels Treaty which, on March 17, 1948—shortly after the Russian *coup d'état* in Prague—created the 'Western Union', has led a rather

THE WESTERN POWERS' VIEW OF THE PROBLEMS

languishing existence, and has been on the whole a planning organization under Field Marshal Montgomery, facing the difficulties in shaping a European Army. But the most recent development into a Western European Union in 1954 has led to important results. This phase must be dealt with in short.

When, in August 1954, the idea of a European Army was rejected, Great Britain felt compelled to leave her former standpoint not to commit herself in questions of purely European defence for a long period of time, and a treaty was signed in London (54) between Belgium, France, Western Germany, Italy, Luxemburg, Holland, Great Britain, Canada and the USA. The occupation of Western Germany was lifted and the Brussels Treaty of 1948 was augmented by the admittance of Western Germany and Italy to membership. The Union established a control organization to see that agreements in the reduction of armaments are honoured and to supervise the export and import of certain types of weapons. The size of stocks of weapons is fixed by the Brussels Treaty Council, with a majority vote and no right of veto. The controlling body, called the Agency for the Control of Armaments, shall ensure that Western Germany obeys certain special regulations. A consultative assembly was also set up by the signatory powers. The USA and Canada inform the Council of the armaments they will contribute.

In return Western Germany pledges not to manufacture atomic, biological, chemical (ABC weapons) or robot weapons within the boundaries of that state.

The whole constitutes an interesting attempt to establish a control organization which can be used as a pattern when the question of world control of conventional and atomic armaments is dealt with. The Brussels control organization does not rely on a large number of supervisors resident at mines, factories and warehouses where weapons are made or stored, but on flying visits to factories and stores, which can be carried out by a smaller number of supervisors.

All defence measures taken by the Western European Union are under the North Atlantic Treaty European command. Thus the whole is a Western European organization for supervision of armaments under the protection of the Atlantic Treaty.

The London treaty was complemented and confirmed in certain respects by the Paris conference of October 20-23. From May 6, 1955, the Western European Union (WEU) is in existence.

With regard to atomic weapons and other armaments, certain special regulations have been drawn up for the Allied troops which remain in Western Germany. Their maximum strength has been fixed, like that of Western Germany (twelve divisions, 1,350 aeroplanes, light vessels for coast defence and escort vessels). Western Germany is allowed to manufacture forbidden weapons only on request of the NATO chief of European defence, and by a two-thirds majority in the Council. But the regulations do not prevent the Western Powers from placing any weapons considered necessary at the disposal of Western Germany. The Western European Union is to have its own budget. The possibilities of standardizing weapons and equipment are to be investigated. A so-called 'armaments pool' is being discussed in the connection.

From this political summary follows a survey of the development of atomic weapons in Great Britain, France and other countries. For reasons of space this survey must be brief, particularly as the most important events in atomic policy have occurred in the USA and have been dealt with above.

THE WESTERN POWERS' VIEW OF THE PROBLEMS

GREAT BRITAIN

Parliamentary debates began and press articles appeared as early as November 1945, but it must be admitted that they often reflected events in the USA, which was the leading country in this sphere. As mentioned above, British atomic research was transferred to America during the latter part of the war. After 1945 the parliamentary debates in Britain showed (56) how the British public wished to protect the interests of the USA, for America was the only country that could help in a new critical situation, but at the same time people were horrified at the idea of atomic bombs being used in a Europe attacked from the East. The Atomic Scientists' Association in Britain led the more technical discussion, while on the political side were the spokesmen of the Government and such people as Bertrand Russell, Lord Hankey, Sir George Thomson, Sir J. Chadwick, Sir John Cockcroft and others (57). Many British scientists have done important work in the USA.

The Atomic Energy Bill (1946) and several other Acts of Parliament regulate the atomic industry. An experimental station with a reactor was opened at Harwell (58) as early as 1947. But it was not until 1952 that the first British atomic bomb was ready to be tested in Australia. Since then production of fissile material has increased. Several large atomic factories exist, and one atomic power station has been constructed at Calder Hall. Twelve more power stations are scheduled for erection in the period 1955-65.

Winston Churchill's 'atomic speech' of March 1, 1955, made it clear that Great Britain intended to make hydrogen bombs of a size not yet specified. Labour has recently declared that Britain cannot be dependent upon any other country in this respect. The British policy is to discourage wars of aggression, which is also the object of this book.

The efficiency of atomic power stations will steadily increase, and the prospect is that in time the cost per unit of electricity from this source will fall relatively until it reaches a figure about the same for that of electricity generated from coal. Up to and including the year 1954 Great Britain has made three atomic bomb tests (October 1952, October 1953 and 1954). The reader is referred to the work 'Britain's Atomic Factories' (58b), which describes the uranium factory at Springfields, the plutonium factory at Windscale and the U 235 factory at Capenhurst under Sir Chr. Hinton. Sir William Penney has become famous for the production of atomic weapons of great explosive force.

Atomic energy research in Britain is directed from Harwell, but the atomic factories are managed from Risley in Lancashire. The uranium mines in Australia, the South African Union and in Canada have increased considerably in importance.

Canada is one of the world's leading countries in the production of uranium, and she was one of the first countries in the world to build atomic piles. Legislation regulating ownership, factory rules, safety and so on was passed in good time. Ever since 1945, therefore, Canada has been represented in the UNAEC. The Atomic Energy Control Board in Ottawa is the central organ for all of Canada's atomic energy problems and publishes periodical reports on the progress made.

FRANCE

In France, which has always taken a humanitarian view in questions of atomic weapons, emphasis was laid right from the beginning on the use of atomic energy for peaceful ends, and an atomic research centre was established at Fort de Chatillon. Prospecting for uranium and thorium was carried on ardently both in France and her colonies.

Three new research centres have been constructed in the neighbourhood of Chatillon, Saclay and Le Bouchet, south of Paris.

There is an extensive French literature dealing with atomic matters. As early as 1950 the official standpoint was clear: prohibition of atomic weapons and strict control.

F. Joliot-Curie, the chairman of the French atomic committee, was a bitter opponent of the atomic bomb, and influenced French opinion greatly (59) in the direction of restraint, while J. Guéron (60) stressed the economic and international legal aspects of the question. Guéron was one of the French delegates to the United Nations AEC. Since Joliot-Curie was replaced by Fr. Perrin as chairman of the French atomic commissariat there has been some irresolution regarding the problem of atomic weapons. In April 1955, however, the Prime Minister, Faure, declared that France herself did not intend to manufacture hydrogen bombs, but all efforts were to be directed towards the application of atomic energy to peaceful ends. As is the case with Western Germany, France can receive atomic weapons from her allies. Political periodicals, which are so important in France, sometimes contain articles (61) on atomic weapons.

France has played an important part in the international attempts to solve the political problems of atomic weapons.

BELGIUM

On account of the great uranium deposits in the Belgian

Congo, an atomic energy commissariat was formed in Belgium in 1951, and several laboratories have been built. The Soviet has tried to buy uranium from the Congo, but the USA has retained the contract. The value of the Congo has increased considerably since uranium was discovered there. Reactors are already being constructed (62). Belgium is included here because of the Belgian Congo.

Information about a large number of countries has recently (1955) been published by the United Nations in a booklet entitled 'Harnessing the Atom for Peace'.

The Supreme Organization of the Western Powers and the Problem of Atomic Weapons

All problems of atomic weapons on the side of the Western Powers must be seen from the point of view of the uniform system created by the North Atlantic Treaty. NATO consists of fifteen states, if Western Germany is included, with a population of about 390,000,000. To these must be added Spain, Yugoslavia and French North Africa, and other countries with which agreements have been signed. Considerable economic and technical help from the USA, the great producer of atomic weapons, is given to the members of the treaty, which naturally influences every country's atomic policy.

SACLANT in Washington makes decisions with regard to atomic problems touching the Atlantic, while those referring to the English Channel are made by CHANCOM in London. Questions dealing with Europe and the Mediterranean come under the authority of SACEUR in the neighbourhood of Paris. In problems of independent strategic air commands, the US Strategic Air Command or the

British Bomber Command is the supreme military instance.

But the great matters of principle such as the possible limitation of atomic weapons and the international standpoint to be taken towards their use, are, naturally, dealt with by the North Atlantic Treaty Council and are the subject of negotiations between representatives of the governments. Thus at the North Atlantic Treaty meeting in Paris, December 18-19, 1954, a number of important questions dealing with atomic weapons were discussed. According to the final report (Le communiqué final), which was published December 19-20, it was asserted that the threat from Russia against the free world had not diminished; a new defence plan for Western Europe, based to a certain extent upon atomic weapons to attain a balance in armaments, was approved, and armament plans were decided; definitive for 1955, provisional for 1956, and planned for 1957.

It is, however, governments or the North Atlantic Council which will decide whether atomic weapons will be used, and the report does not distinguish between large and small, so-called tactical, atomic weapons. The political authorities, therefore, retain full responsibility to authorize action. The procedure leading to a decision shall be further studied by the NATO Council representatives in Paris, after which the proposal is remitted to the governments. In spite of that, Dulles declared on December 22, 1954, that the NATO commander-in-chief had the right to use atomic artillery in order to attain sufficient firing power, and President Eisenhower gave reasons why the right of retaliation must be safeguarded.

Care is taken not to betray any details, for the Soviet shows no signs of doing so, and there are many indications that a decision will be kept secret so that the Soviet will not easily be able to work out how much time it will take before a decision is arrived at, and calculate the advantages of attacking first.

But no veto seems able to prevent a Western Power from using atomic weapons in its defence if attacked. This is in accordance with the wishes of the USA to have free hands with regard to the use of the strategic bomber force.

At the same time as the council meeting mentioned above, protective measures to be taken in case of a bomb attack were discussed, and it was resolved to establish a technical central organization in The Hague for the air defence of the Western Powers; this organization is under the supervision of SHAPE.

A war with atomic weapons, therefore, is not inevitable, provided that no power begins a war of offence with either conventional or atomic weapons.

Konrad Adenauer stated in December 1954 that the decisive question is whether a solution can be found to the problem of the control of atomic weapons or not. If a solution is found there will be a relaxation of tension; if not, the race for armaments and a consequent increase of tension will be the result.

After the ratification of the Paris Treaty, Western Germany became a member of the North Atlantic Treaty, German rearmament was begun and the new control of military armaments (p. 59–60) came in to force.

With reference to the total superiority of the Western Powers it should be remembered that in the Far East, the SEATO treaty binds the USA, Great Britain, Australia and New Zealand, together with Pakistan, Siam and the Philippine Islands, to mutual defence against open attack. With this end in view, common defence forces with small atomic weapons have been organized.

Chapter 5

THE EASTERN POWERS' VIEW OF THE PROBLEMS

THE SOVIET

The Soviet 1945-50

The student of the political development of the problem of atomic weapons in the Soviet has far fewer sources at his disposal than are to be found on the side of the Western Powers. Even so, documents from the Soviet are so numerous as to compel the author to make a very strict selection of the source material dealing with atomic energy (atomnaja jadernaja energija) and the atomic bomb (atomnaja bomba). On the other hand, Russian literature is poor in detailed, official works of the kind that are so numerous in the Western world—the reports of all the official commissions and parliamentary debates.

Stalin and his Home Secretary, Beria, kept atomic problems behind double iron curtains!

There is a rather comprehensive description of atomic problems from the Russian point of view in the third edition of 'Balchaija sovjetskaja entsiklopedia' (Great Soviet Encyclopedia (63)), the third part of which contains eighty pages dealing with different aspects of the atomic problem. There is much valuable information to be gleaned there, with, however, two reservations. The first is that this official description is much amplified by information on the part played by Engels, Lenin and Stalin in the creation of atomic weapons, while all that has been done in the West, particularly since 1932, is kept in the distant background. The second is that the volume of the Encyclopedia containing this information was printed in 1950, before the advent of the hydrogen bomb. But there is much of interest on the preceding period. Valuable information has occasionally appeared in Russian periodicals (64).

Last, but not least, the sources mentioned as special literature (111-118) have been of great value in the study of the uranium deposits of the Soviet.

The first statement made by Stalin about the atomic bomb was in 1945, but he did not attribute any great importance to it, which was understandable, for then Russia had no atomic bombs, and the public had to be reassured. But soon after the end of the war the Soviet standpoint in the question of atomic weapons was expressed by Stalin, who, at the end of 1946, told an American journalist that atomic energy should be subject to strict international control (65). At that time the USA had a great advantage over the Soviet as far as atomic bombs were concerned, but, as became evident later, Russia had already begun secret experiments herself. In May 1947, Stalin discussed with H. Stassen, the American statesman, the possibility of creating an international control organization (66), and on the thirty-first anniversary of the October Revolution Molotov stressed the necessity of prohibiting the use of atomic weapons (67). This became the guiding theme for the whole Russian press and the press in the satellite states during the following years, and the theme was often accentuated by the assertion that prohibition and control of atomic weapons were essential for real peace in the world. On the diplomatic front Gromyko was given the task of making propaganda for the same point of view, and of explaining the attitude of the Soviet towards the question of control (68). As a preliminary the USA plan for control (the Baruch Plan) was adversely criticized, as was

THE EASTERN POWERS' VIEW OF THE PROBLEMS

the suggestion that the Soviet should give up the right of veto (69). When foreign writers, including Joliot-Curie in France, described the devastation caused by an atomic war, their accounts were given great prominence in the Russian press. From the Soviet point of view the blockade of Berlin was a reply to the Marshall Plan.

In May the Russians extended the blockade of Berlin to the highway and canal, and the language of the Soviet press was full of invectives. In the meantime efforts to realize Vyshinsky's plan to unite the Eastern European states in an alliance were intensified, while at the same time the USA was depicted as the country really preventing the control of atomic weapons (78). When the Western Powers organized the air bridge to break the blockade, the Soviet felt her inferiority in atomic weapons and feared to render the situation more acute. This was a bitter lesson for the atomic experts of the Soviet Union! After the General Assembly meeting in 1948 the Soviet press was loud in its praises of Russia's desire to come to a result, while the USA was represented as unwilling (71). The Moscow weekly, *New Times*, devoted a series of articles to this highly topical subject (72), and towards the close of 1948 the waves of controversy ran high. The private opinions of American citizens, that the USA must be prepared for an atomic war, were used with great advantage. Even statements by former members of the Soviet delegation to the atomic energy commissions (73) were cited. The authority of U. Zhukov was enlisted against the principle line of policy pursued by the USA (74), and the press of the satellite countries, particularly that of Poland, echoed these sentiments (75).

The Soviet press tried to ignore the value of the North Atlantic Treaty when it was ratified by France in July 1949.

INTERNATIONAL ATOMIC POLICY

Events in 1949 led to the breaking of the silence surrounding the atomic investigations of the Soviet. Articles were published on the principles of nuclear reactors (jaderny reaktor), the significance of chemical mines for certain materials (chimitjesky savodyi) and the meaning of the conception fission (djelenije jadra). Articles dealing with the different kinds of raw materials (syirje), particularly uranium (oran) and thorium (torij) and the risk of radioactive contamination (radioaktivnost) round the sites of atomic bomb tests and factories—all in anticipation of the completion of the Russian atomic bomb. Malik, the Soviet representative at the meeting of the General Assembly in 1949, took up the offensive against the USA, who had proposed the Baruch Plan. The Soviet was against this plan from the outset, and represented it as an attempt by America to monopolize all the uranium mines in the world.

TASS announced on September 25, 1949, that extensive works were proceeding in the USSR. Electric power stations were being built, new mines opened up, canals and roads were being constructed, all of which demanded the application of all up-to-date technical means, including atomic energy. The public were told not to be uneasy. TASS announced that in August a Russian atomic bomb, on which work was commenced in 1947, had been exploded, and that this was a continuation of the experimental bombs made during the years 1947-48. Its explosive power was said to be six times as great as that of the Hiroshima bomb. Since September 23 people in the USA knew about this test because a message was given from the Western side. At the same time, the Soviet insisted on the prohibition of the atomic bomb (76).

In November 1949, Molotov asserted that American 'atomic diplomacy' was based on the mistaken assumption that the Soviet had no atomic bombs (77). And Voroshilov declared that the Soviet had long had atomic bombs of her own (78). A few days later Molotov underlined this in an election speech in the Tashkent-Lenin constituency, where he said that the Soviet's enemies had formerly threatened the land with atomic bombs, but now it was the hydrogen bomb, which, however, was not yet completed. But the Soviet had not rested on her laurels, and was now in command of the secrets of atomic energy (79). Minister Kaganovich added in an election speech that industry in the Soviet was well equipped for atomic problems, thanks to the foresight of the Party and Stalin himself. Now was the time to make atomic energy help to build up and defend Communism (80).

The mighty Russian institution known as Agitprop—agitation and propaganda—was by that time prepared for a new mission. In June 1950 the Soviet Government issued a declaration in accordance with the appeal for peace, which the curious 'Stockholm Conference' with its 'Stockholm Appeal' advocated, and announced the peaceful intentions of the Soviet (81). It was at that time, when the world situation was characterized by the outbreak of war in Korea, that the Soviet completed her atomic bomb and the USA was on the way to the hydrogen bomb. At the same time the affair of Klaus Fuchs in the USA and the espionage in Canada showed that the Soviet was eager to keep in touch with developments in the USA.

The Stockholm Appeal of 1950 was used in the Soviet as anti-American propaganda. Among those who took part were A. Moskvin and T. D. Lysenko, the authors, a number of well-known journalists from *Pravda*, *Izvestia*, *New Times* (82) and *Soviet Monitor*, to mention only a few, and a number of communist journalists abroad. All this was given a kind of backward surge when it reached the

American public and resulted in rather violent discussions, even among international atomic specialists, many of whom were hesitant in face of the development that atomic weapons were forcing upon mankind.

The circumstance that the United Nations AEC had ceased work in December 1949—the Western Powers had found the work fruitless—caused a storm of indignation in Russian literature and the press. At the beginning of 1950 the principal theme of Soviet propaganda was as follows: prohibit atomic weapons as weapons of offence, establish strict control and brand as war criminals the first government to make use of such weapons (84).

Propaganda for the peaceful application of atomic energy was started at the same time in the Soviet. The future secretary of the party, N. S. Kruschev, the electro-specialist G. Krhishanovsky, M. Rubenstein and many others took part, clearly inspired by the government, in the debate. V. Matvejev complained that the great American capitalists were opposed to the use of atomic energy for peaceful purposes, for it was an undesirable rival to coal, oil and electricity, while TASS reiterated that atomic fissions were taking place in connection with the establishment of new electricity generating plants, in mines and in canal construction. All this was effectively contrasted to the repeated atomic bomb tests in the USA. Russian propaganda in *Pravda* (May 13, 1950), 'Vyiche snamja borbyi za mir!' (Raise the battle-flag for peace!) echoed through press and propaganda. There were propaganda explosions in real atomic style.

New attacks on the USA by the Soviet followed President Truman's declaration that America intended to continue experiments with a hydrogen bomb, and after the Western Powers had created a unified North Atlantic Treaty command, Russian hate became white hot.

THE EASTERN POWERS' VIEW OF THE PROBLEMS

Russian proceedings with regard to atomic weapons showed clear tendencies towards increased technical efforts after the USA began the manufacture of hydrogen bombs. This was also reflected in propaganda, which accused America of turning the development of atomic materials into military channels (85), and it was claimed in the Soviet that President Truman had come to a decision in opposition to American, French, British and other scientists (86). Which, as is now known, was only partly true. Several Russian atomic experts showed in scientific and political literature that it was certainly not the Soviet that prevented the prohibition of atomic weapons by rejecting the control plans formulated by the Western Powers. In this connection much prominence was given to the fact that the Baruch Plan assumed that an international syndicate should own all the mines in the world where fissionable material were produced, which was unimaginable for Russian mentality.

During the whole of this period of discussion, the Soviet was preparing to help North Korea in the war that broke out on June 25.

In July 1950 the US Atomic Energy Commission dealt with the problem of the hydrogen bomb and its connection with the control of atomic energy, and in the Soviet, plans were made how to meet this new situation. A peace organization in the USA put certain questions to Y. A. Malik, the Soviet representative to the United Nations. In September he gave a rather comprehensive reply in which he stressed the Russian view of the importance of a total prohibition of atomic weapons (78). The spokesmen of peace organizations, particularly the second congress of the World Peace Council, dwelt in considerable detail on the danger of atomic bombs, and influenced opinion in the whole world. A. Y. Vyshinsky, as a member of the Government in Moscow, received a deputation of American women and promised that the Soviet would honour an agreement for the prohibition of atomic weapons, and in Washington Malik took care of the Trade Unionists' Conference and the Women's Committee, besides other associations working in America for the promotion of peace (88). The whole was a large scale propaganda offensive which was carried on at the same time as bloody battles were being fought in Korea.

The Soviet 1951-52

In 1951 Stalin himself granted an interview to *Pravda* to refute Attlee's (then Prime Minister) claim in the House of Commons that the Soviet had not reduced, but increased her armaments since the war (89). These statements were commented upon in newspapers all over the world, and in the Russian press, which also gave a summary of what had been said on the subject in about twenty other countries. It was naturally stressed strongly by Russia that America was the great enemy of peace in the world. At the end of 1951 Russia made her second atomic bomb test.

All this was received with approval by certain persons in the USA, where, in the *Bulletin of Atomic Scientists*, two atomic specialists maintained that an agreement must soon be reached to prohibit atomic weapons before the stocks became very large. In October Stalin found it expedient to make a statement on the Russian atomic bomb tests, and to demand the prohibition of atomic bombs and a control which, however, was not to interfere too radically in the autonomy of any state (90).

Russia's new Five-Year Plan, which began in 1951, was mainly concerned with heavy industries and goods necessary in case of war.

THE EASTERN POWERS' VIEW OF THE PROBLEMS

The year 1952 opened with a number of diplomatic conferences, including a four power committee in Paris, convened by the United Nations General Assembly, where the Soviet, for political reasons, gave a somewhat more conciliatory tune in the question of the control of atomic energy. But no practical results were arrived at, and no decisions were made. It became increasingly evident that the Soviet made use of agents in foreign countries, particularly in the USA, to obtain information about America's hydrogen bomb. With regard to the Korean war, the Stalinists were of the opinion that it would help to exhaust the Western Powers, while Malenkov and the Reformists considered that it would stimulate them to increased armaments to the disadvantage of the Soviet.

At the close of the year Malenkov analysed the whole of the international situation, disarmament negotiations and the prohibition of atomic weapons (91), generally speaking on conventional lines. But it was not until the following year Molotov announced that the Soviet had solved the technical problems connected with the construction of the hydrogen bomb. It was America's new president, Eisenhower, who received the Russian tidings.

The Soviet 1953

Stalin died in March, a new regime under Malenkov took over, and Beria's fall set new rumours in circulation. Exceptional interest in the new leaders was manifested abroad. Would the Soviet standpoint in the problems of atomic weapons and their control undergo any change? A study of the new regime was made by the present author, dealing with the likelihood of a change in Russian policy (92). The satellite states were also the subject of a similar investigation (93). The conclusion arrived at was that, as far as foreign affairs were concerned, little departure could be expected from Stalin's policy, which was dominated by the policy of Russian expansion combined with the salvation of the world through Communism. But it was stressed at the same time that within the Soviet Union the old Stalinists were counteracted by the so-called Reformists, who, led by Malenkov, were probably of the opinion that a period of peace and reduced political tension was necessary for the Soviet Union, in order to raise somewhat the very low standard of living which was causing much dissatisfaction among large parts of the population, particularly in the satellite states. It is from this point of view that the change in Russia's atomic policy which occurred a little later, and which is dealt with at the end of Chapter 3 above, took place.

The new Russian regime showed no signs of wavering when the disturbances in Berlin and Eastern Germany were subdued with Stalinist severity. At the same time the Soviet Union showed increased willingness to negotiate, and advised the People's Republic of China to wind up the war in Korea. In 1953 an agreement was reached to hold a Foreign Ministers' Conference at the beginning of the following year (in Berlin), where the questions of atomic weapons and armaments would be discussed. In the meantime, in August, the Soviet Union exploded her first hydrogen bomb, probably stationary, not from an aeroplane. At the end of 1953 *Pravda* (December 22) declared that the Soviet Union was in favour of strict international control and the prohibition of atomic weapons in warfare. The development of the international situation was rather unfavourable for Russian foreign policy, for there was no split in the Western Powers. Stalin's theory that a war would break out between the capitalistic powers seemed more and more unrealistic. But that did not deter the

THE EASTERN POWERS' VIEW OF THE PROBLEMS

Soviet Union from working to isolate the USA from the other Western Powers and to increase tension between France and Western Germany (94). The Russian press often asserted that the problem of atomic weapons must be seen in the light of the fact that the USA and a stronger Western Germany were the worst enemies of peace.

The USA became known in Russia by the appellation 'The transoceanic aggressor' (zaokeanisky agressor). The Soviet Union was not adverse to making statements in the name of Europe when the production of hydrogen bombs was begun and she felt stronger.

The Soviet Union 1954-55

In connection with what was said in Chapter 3 about the general situation it need only be mentioned here (95) that an announcement on April 1 to the effect that Russia had no objections to becoming a member of the Atlantic Treaty was not really taken seriously in the Western world. The Russian press hailed the Geneva Conference on Korea and Indo-China as a great Russian success, for then, for the first time, the People's Republic of China was represented at a conference of the Great Powers, and in addition the communist advance in Indo-China could be continued with suitable means. When the EDC proposal was rejected there was jubilation in Russia, and the new London-Paris agreement was opposed diligently.

Round the close of the year 1954 Russian propaganda was mainly occupied with the theme that those who are against negotiations with the Soviet Union in European affairs prevent the reunion of Western and Eastern Germany. But the Western Powers held the opinion that only after a consolidation of the West could the question of the reunion of Germany be taken up with any hope of success.

The Russian press opposed this view bitterly. It was one of the aims of Russian policy to ensure that the situation in Germany did not change to their disadvantage.

The American hydrogen bomb tests had powerful repercussions in the Soviet Union, and much publicity was given to Dulle's statement that the USA must meet aggression with atomic weapons. The threat of atomic bombs is used in Russia to bind the satellite states with still tighter bands, which is justified by a common air defence. But at the same time fatalism is held in check among the people by emphasizing the greater significance of conventional weapons. However, a propaganda campaign was begun during the autumn to spread information of the effect of the hydrogen bomb, at the same time as the Soviet Union (as mentioned in Chapter 3) accepted the British-French compromise as a basis for negotiations.

The Bulganin-Kruschev-Zhukov regime has spoken in favour of a conference of the Great Powers, and in an interview Kruschev has stated that the principle of the balance of power is a good one, but threats were made to cancel the Non-aggression Treaty with Great Britain and France, and speed up the production of atomic weapons. Those treaties have been cancelled by the Soviet during 1955.

Some words about the atomic industry and legislation in the Soviet Union are necessary. Two Russians succeeded in splitting uranium atoms in 1940, with the help of information they had received from German institutes, but then the demands of war made further progress very difficult. There are many signs that the Soviet Union had succeeded in making a kind of atomic bomb by 1947-48, that is, more than a year before the Soviet Government and President Truman announced that Russia was in possession of the bomb. The first explosion of a large atomic bomb perhaps took place prematurely on account of faulty safety devices and caused casualties among the personnel. There is a special department of the Ministry for Internal Affairs (MVD) which has long had the task of guarding the secrets of the Soviet Union's atomic energy experiments. Three underground towns, Atomgrad 1, 2 and 3, have been built and explosion tests have been made in the Karaku Desert to the east of the Caspian Sea. Advantage was taken of the experience gained by the above-mentioned accident, and since July 1949 the Soviet Union is considered to have mastered the scientific prevention of accidents.

Professor S. P. Alexandrov was a member of the United Nations AEC for several years, and was present at the American tests at Bikini in 1946. But certain important points were not included in the Smyth report of 1945, among other things the proportions of the materials comprising the bomb. The Russian atomic energy commission under the auspices of the Soviet Union Academy of Science under L. Beria, the chief of the secret police, was augmented by a number of German scientists, and a special intelligence service under the above-mentioned Alexandrov was engaged in obtaining technical information from abroad. Groups of scientists under the president of the academy, S. I. Vavilov, were engaged in completing the atomic towns, and an extensive organization was created to prospect for uranium deposits. The best-known Russian atomic specialists are P. Kapitsa, Joffe, Chlopin and Krichanovsky. Among the fifty or so German experts may be mentioned Professor G. Hertz, who was a specialist on uranium. It is not yet known to whom should be given the honour of having finally solved the problem of constructing the bomb, but it is very probable that it occurred thanks both to scientific research carried out by more than 300 specialists and to leakages from the Western Powers. There is no confirmation that the Soviet Union's bomb produces an explosion of only of medium size.

Nuclear research in the USSR was concentrated for a long time to institutes in Leningrad and Kharkov, but atomic bombs were made in Caucasus. It should be observed that there are many different versions, but the following may be considered—on the whole—as reliable, with the exception of some few details. Eight great atomic centres gradually developed (Appendices 2 and 3):

1. In Caucasus with some mines and Atomgrad 1,
2. In the Ural Mountains with several mines and Atomgrad 2,
3. In Ferghana, north of the Pamir Plateau, with Atomgrad 3 (Tuyuya Muyun),
4. In Tannu Tuva with a number of mines and atomic factories,
5. By Lake Baikal,
6. In the gold mines of northern Siberia,
7. In Transbaikal, and
8. To the north east of Transbaikal.

To these may possibly be added Alma Ata in Kazakstan. There are now more than 800 institutions with a staff of over 40,000 working on different aspects of atomic problems. Both the manufacture of atomic bombs and the peaceful use of atomic energy enjoy much support from the state and the authorities (96). During 1954-55 large bodies of people are being moved from other parts of the Soviet to the area along the chain of uranium mines in southern Siberia. The economic crisis in the Soviet is an obstacle, however.

As Gordon Dean (97) points out, the expansion of the atomic industry and the increase in atomic weapons fac-

THE EASTERN POWERS' VIEW OF THE PROBLEMS

tories should not be disregarded or underrated. On the contrary much hard work is being done there. But the Russian system of communicating but little of what has happened has created an impression that attempts were made to belittle the threat of atomic weapons as long as Russia was behind in the race. The USA, however, has always been rather well informed of events in the Soviet Union.

It is not the writer's intention to describe Russian industry, but a few points should be mentioned.

Large amounts of uranium have been discovered, thanks to the work of the prospecting commissions, which included Professor Smirnov and Fersman, a geologist. There are first-class uranium mines in Czechoslovakia and Saxony, and the total uranium deposits of the Soviet Union are comparable with those of the USA. Cobalt and a large number of other metals are to be found in the Urals. (Cf. Appendices 2 and 3.) It may be that the Soviet Union's much strained Five-Year Plans have seldom been realized, but they give the authorities the possibility of making plans covering several financial years. Fuel, electric power, iron and steel are sufficient for an atomic weapon programme. P. Kapitza, who has lived in England and is a famous specialist, was given in 1935 a high post as one of the leaders of the Soviet's atomic research work. Politics has great influence over science, and even scientists must be careful what they say.

According to the Russians the first cyclotron in Europe was built in Moscow (!), and experiments with uranium fissions were made in 1939. The scientific periodicals increased in numbers and value. The financial side of all institutions is centralized in the Academy of Science. Much help was obtained by means of espionage in the West, but purely Russian research and improved technical training enabled the Soviet to solve the problem herself, says Gordon Dean, who when he was chairman of the US Atomic Energy Commission was in a good position to survey the chances of the Soviet Union in the race for superiority in atomic weapons. He has come to the conclusion that the Soviet Union has the essential requirements for the production of atomic weapons, and that the USA must increase her efforts if she is to keep the lead. Gordon Dean bases his statements partly on the authority of atomic experts who have resided in Russia.

Appendices 2 and 3 show that the Western Powers have access to far greater deposits of ores from which the materials for atomic and hydrogen bombs can be extracted. There is no doubt whatsoever that the mines of the USA, Canada, the Belgian Congo and the South African Union yield much more than those of Russia and China, and that the total industrial resources of the Western Powers which can be harnessed to the production of atomic weapons are much greater. Is that not a good reason for the Soviet to accept a cessation of the production of the large hydrogen and atomic weapons?

THE SATELLITE STATES

Questions of atomic energy and atomic weapons in the satellite states of the Soviet Union must be seen against the background of the political and industrial development of these countries and their dependence upon the Soviet Union.

In the existing situation, as long as the partition of Germany is in force, Eastern Germany must be reckoned as a satellite state in the same way as Albania, Bulgaria, Rumania, Czechoslovakia and Hungary. Esthonia, Latvia, Lithuania, Western Karelia, the eastern part of

THE EASTERN POWERS' VIEW OF THE PROBLEMS

Poland, the eastern corner of Rumania and Carpathian-Ukraine are incorporated into various parts of the Soviet Union system of sixteen republics (98).

Outer Mongolia, Tannu Tuva, north-west of Mongolia, the republic of East Sinkiang and possibly parts of Manchuria in Asia belong to a similar group of states (99). According to the Statesman's Year Book (1954), there are in addition in Asia six 'independent regions' and twelve 'independent republics' of a more limited extent, which have a varying character of colonial satellite states (100).

This shows that the Soviet Union finds it advantageous in very large areas within her boundaries to surround herself with nominally independent countries which are in reality dependent upon the Soviet Union in almost all respects. In this way the fiction that these states are independent is kept up, while the USSR govern them more or less strictly as occasion demands. This system allows the Soviet Union to infiltrate into countries bordering upon the satellite states without being made responsible. The Soviet has also the possibility of remaining 'neutral' in so-called 'civil wars', which are calculated to advance the aims of the world revolution. This is the vital point which will reconcile Russian imperialism with the Communist conquest of the world.

The six Eastern European satellite states mentioned above have together more than 71,000,000 inhabitants—with Eastern Germany 88,000,000. Even if Russia's methods in the vassal states must be criticized and many shortcomings exist, it must be admitted that the production of these countries is increased in every possible way, particularly that of industry, with which this work is concerned (101). But the satellite states have thus become more valuable to the Soviet Union, for the European vassal states alone have together a production of raw materials amounting to almost one-third of that of the whole Soviet Union (98).

From this may be gathered, as is often confirmed by the press in the satellite states, that the Soviet Union has become more interested in the military protection of the industries of the satellite states. Russian propaganda plays with advantage on the threat of atomic weapons which the Western Powers can direct against them and their people, and conjures forth the wish for greater protection by Russian forces of all kinds. This facilitates the pro-Russian political and military leadership of the satellite states, where the Russian secret police have succeeded in liquidating practically all the more important centres of resistance. The people, however, are for good reasons against a war of aggression (102), but of course, a complicated situation may arise on account of a so-called 'civil war' in the boundary areas.

The policy of the Western Powers in the satellite states has changed from merely attempting to prevent the further expansion of the Soviet Union to a so-called policy of liberation without war, in which it is hoped that the development of Western democracy and ideals of freedom, together with a parliamentary system, will be so attractive to Eastern Europe that the satellite system will be weakened (103).

Isolated from the Western world as they are, the satellite states cannot count upon any help from the West to develop their atomic industries, but possibly, in case of war between East and West, that the Western Powers drop their bombs on the Soviet Union proper and not on the satellite states.

For many years the Soviet has delivered radioactive isotopes for research and medical use to the satellite states, and resolved in 1955 to construct atomic piles and cyclo-

THE EASTERN POWERS' VIEW OF THE PROBLEMS

trons for peaceful uses in Poland, Czechoslovakia, Rumania, Eastern Germany and possibly in Bulgaria and Hungary, and to train the personnel for these installations. The atomic industry is in close connection with other industries (104), so a little must be said about those, too.

The Russian system, of 1946-48, of moving stocks, railway material and other transport material from the 'liberated' countries as well as whole industrial plants, has been succeeded by a system of encouraging the expansion of industrial production under strong centralized Russian leadership, even if agriculture is thereby neglected. For that reason, many of the satellite states are dependent upon Russian cereals, while industrial products have to be sold in the USSR. Heavy industries, financed by the Eastern 'Marshall Plan', are organized to provide the goods that are lacking in the Soviet Union, according to five-year-plans approved by the Soviet Union for each state (101). Collaboration is organized through a body usually called 'Komekon', which, under the Russian Board of Trade, plans the whole economy of the Russian sphere of influence. From the Russian inspectors in the uranium mines of the satellite states by way of Russian advisers in the so-called mixed companies or the completely state-owned factories right to the top of the pyramid, the Soviet Union makes the decisions. The case is the same with regard to atomic weapons. Appendices 2 and 3 show how much is now known on the basis of non-secret sources about uranium mines and the like.

As these areas are enveloped in secrecy, it is difficult to obtain all the facts, but so much is clear that the Soviet is working all mines where uranium is to be found, manufacturing atomic bombs in enclosed areas in the Soviet Union, and lending smaller atomic weapons to fully reliable satellite states. It must not be forgotten that the large atomic weapons make it possible for the Soviet Union to bring pressure to bear upon potential oppositional satellites and their neighbours if necessary. This has probably some influence on Russian policy.

The great industrial resources of the satellite states, mostly already 'nationalized', have been of great advantage to the Soviet Union and increased the ability of the Eastern Powers to become self supporting. (The sources give in Appendix 1, Nos. 111-18, provide a good basis for forming an estimate of this.)

The uranium mines of Czechoslovakia (cf. Appendices 2 and 3), above all those at Joachimsthal, and coal, iron and copper are important to a very considerable armaments industry. All deposits of fissionable material are being exploited to the full. The oil and metals of Albania and Rumania, the latter country's chemicals, Bulgaria's heavy industries and the uranium mines at Gotenberg and Stara Zagora, Poland's uranium mine, Lysa Gora, coal, steel and oil, and the mines of Hungary are great assets for the Soviet Union (101, 105, 106). Occupied Eastern Germany contributes with about twenty uranium mines, many of which are worked by the 'Industrial Department of the Soviet Ministry of War'.

The natural resources of Asia are of enormous significance to the atomic industry of the Soviet Union, and many deposits lie within the boundaries of Russia. The republics of Kazakstan and Tadzhikistan to the east of the Caspian Sea, have, as has Siberia, rich uranium and other mines (107). But the Asiatic satellites have large supplies, too.

In Outer Mongolia, with which state the Soviet made a Treaty of Defence in 1936 and which by a plebiscite in 1945 became a nominally independent state, but where the Soviet Union in reality rules, are many valuable min-

THE EASTERN POWERS' VIEW OF THE PROBLEMS

erals. The same is the case in Tannu Tuva, which was occupied by Russia in 1945 and later made into an 'independent region'. There are several large atomic factories there. South Sakhalin and the Kurile Islands, which were also gained in 1945, are not so important, but the harbour of Dairen is of great significance. The position of Port Arthur is dealt with below in connection with the People's Republic of China.

The Soviet Union was granted a privileged position in Manchuria in 1945. The railways are administered in co-operation with China and there has been a combined Russian-Chinese military command. Iron, oil and metals are to be found, and uranium in the southern part. The northern part of Sinkiang has been divided from the rest and the republic of East Sinkiang, which is really a Russian vassal, established. The Soviet Union has the right to exploit the uranium mines in West Sinkiang (atomic factory at Thiwa). Finally, Russian influence in North Korea and Viet-nam is accompanied by certain advantages.

For all these satellites, as for Asiatic Russia in its entirety, the enormous areas make effective air-defence impossible, and the American air-bases from Alaska via Japan and Pakistan to Turkey are naturally irritating for people at the Russian atomic mines and atomic factories.

As far as can be seen, the Soviet Union seems to have succeeded in creating a rather large degree of affinity with China, even with regard to the Soviet's Asiatic satellites. It is interesting to observe that when Mao Tse-tung on all suitable occasions sends greetings to the Soviet's satellite states he does not forget the former Chinese, and present Russian, provincial republics in the Far East. Formally the satellite states are treated as if they were equal to the Soviet, a state of affairs that is emphasized by skilful propaganda. M. Fainsod, of Cambridge, recently published a book on how the Soviet Union is governed, and he shows clearly how the authorities, party organizations and the police, work together in the satellite states, too (108).

It is true that the Russian regime 1953-54, with Malenkov at its head instead of Stalin, took great pains not to offend the satellites, but the Russian policy towards these states showed no tendency to allow them greater freedom. President Voroshilov said, too, at the end of 1953, that Russia would retain her hold on the satellite states and not surrender her influence on the future of Germany. The Bulganin-Kruschev-Zhukov regime has declared that certain federal states shall be allowed to have their own defence departments. It is at present uncertain whether this will mean more power for the military leaders.

Unfortunately atomic weapons have given Russia the possibility of increasing her power with means that do not always require the occupation of a country. As long as the Soviet Union retains this possibility, the Western Powers will hardly renounce the right to make use of atomic weapons against aggression, but the problem will be who is to decide if aggression has really taken place.

It is well known that experiences of infiltration wars are not very encouraging.

Legislation in Russia, contrary to the case in other countries, is available only within certain limits. There are many 'reports' (dokladyi) from which only few important facts can be gathered, while the iron curtain is impenetrable as far as special laws and decrees are concerned. As, on principle, no secret sources have been used in this book, Russian legislation must, unfortunately be passed over. Even the voluminous United Nations 'Bibliography' has hardly any source material on Russian legislation dealing with atomic problems, while that of other countries is

THE EASTERN POWERS' VIEW OF THE PROBLEMS

treated in detail. Much is due to the fact that atomic factories in Russia are situated in so-called closed areas and that the curtain is extra impenetrable there.

In conclusion it must be mentioned that a network of political agreements connect not only the satellites with Russia but also the satellites with each other (109, 110).

Russia's total resources of ores from which fissile material can be won have been determined rather accurately with the help of Russian and other sources, which are given in Appendix 1, Nos. 64-110, and the special literature included in Nos. 111-18.

THE PEOPLE'S REPUBLIC OF CHINA

The People's Republic of China, whose new constitution was adopted on June 14, 1954, belongs to the Eastern Powers in so far as mutual antagonism unites them against the Western Powers, to which must be added the communist philosophy created more than thirty years ago by Russian teachers (119). A socialist state has been built up methodically since the revolution in China was brought to a close in 1949, founded on the experiences gained during the war of the revolution (120). With its 601,000,000 inhabitants—three times as many as in Russia—China claims to be a completely independent state with the same rights as Russia, even if the People's Republic is, and will continue for a long time to be, greatly dependent upon Russia in many ways.

From the political point of view, the 1950 pacts—signed in February, while the Korean war began in June—form the basis of the relationship between these two great powers. Their object is friendship, alliance and mutual help on the basis of 'equality, mutual advantage and respect for the sovereignty and territory of each state'

(121). Taking everything into consideration, these pacts are based on community of interests (122) and are in keeping with Stalin's idea as expressed in his last statements, that a Russian-Chinese dominion should be formed, which would be impossible to overthrow.

The political bonds were strengthened by agreements to hold periodical conferences (123): to get the People's Republic elected to the UN, to unite Korea, to condemn the South-East Asian Military Alliance organized by the Western Powers, and to prevent the rearmament of Japan under the leadership of the USA. Exchanges of parliamentary delegations, large exhibitions to stimulate collaboration and co-ordinate political propaganda strengthen the ties (124).

The economic bands are strong indeed. Trade between the two countries is increasing rapidly. Russia has financed and will continue to finance China, who was hard hit economically by the Korean war. In accordance with a resolution in parliament in October 1954 (125), the USSR will help to build up China's industry, and draw up five-year plans with the help of Russian military and industrial advisers. The Chinese Prime Minister, Chou En-lai, said in parliament on September 23, 1954 (126) that of 600 new factories, Russia would build 141 for heavy industries and the production of arms, among other things. The mixed Chinese-Russian companies that existed earlier have been wound up, and all industry is now the property of the Chinese state. A number of railways are being built in common.

Military collaboration, which has been very strong for several decades, has been further increased. There has been at times a common command in Manchuria; Russian military advisers have been seen all over China, even in the southern parts (127); Russian instructors and Russian arms are to be found in all Chinese provinces, as in the Russian satellite states, and the Soviet Union is making great efforts to increase the military strength of the People's Republic. Certain observers claim that Russia does not want China to become too strong, but wants China to be dependent on Russia for a long time to come. A Soviet-Chinese military commission at Port Arthur is, according to a recent agreement, due to be dissolved in May 1955, when Russian troops have begun to withdraw from the Port Arthur district. There are some military observers who consider that China will need military help for another generation. But the eternal civil wars and the recent Korean war show that the Chinese make good soldiers (128). The development of atomic weapons may be expected to increase China's dependence upon Russia.

In view of the above, it is clear that the development of atomic energy will have great influence on the future of Asia, where collaboration between China and Russia is very intimate. Since October 1954 there has existed a joint scientific-technical organization consisting of seven members from each country. Meetings are held alternately in Moscow and Peking (118). Only atom-powered industrial plants are mentioned in the Chinese press, but it is certain (126) that China wishes to make tactical atomic weapons for her own use. Certain circumstances in the Korean war must be taken into consideration in this connection.

M. Beloff says in his very informative work, 'Soviet Policy in the Far East' (119), that there is no doubt that it was thanks to help from Russia that the Chinese Revolution was successful during the years 1948-49, that the Soviet Union trained the whole of the North Korean Army and supplied it with modern weapons and equipment, and Koreans who had been living in Russia. But at the same time, he considers that it cannot be historically proved that Russia started the Korean war at a time chosen by Russia. Other experts on Asiatic questions claim that Stalin and Mao Tse-tung planned the Korean war at their meeting in Moscow at the beginning of 1950.

This brings us to another point of view which the development of atomic weapons has brought about. It was not known then, but we know now, that *it was in Aug.–Sept. 1949 that Russia exploded her first atomic bomb, so that from the spring of 1950 the Soviet Union was not in the same inferior position as earlier, but could play for higher stakes.* The Korean war was extremely favourable for Russia. A large proportion of the military forces of the Western Powers was tied up in the Far East, and after China had been induced to intervene against the Western Powers the Korean war became a powerful means of sowing hate between the People's Republic of China and the United Nations forces, provided by the Western Powers.

The Korean war began on June 25, 1950, and finished on July 27, 1953. The first period was favourable for the UN forces, but after Chinese communist armies intervened in October 1950 the UN forces suffered serious set-backs in November and December. Great pressure was then brought to bear on the government of the USA to make use of the atomic bomb. The fact that the Soviet Union also had atomic bombs was a deterrent. In January 1951 the situation was stabilized. From the historical-political point of view it cannot be said that the UN was victorious, for the result of the armistice was a demilitarized zone, north of latitude 38. Of course one may say, with Adlai E. Stevenson in America (129), that the European West would perhaps never have armed if America had not taken the lead in Korea, and that the action encouraged the idea of collective security. But an expansion of the Korean war into

THE EASTERN POWERS' VIEW OF THE PROBLEMS

a great war was inexpedient since the Soviet Union had the atomic bomb too. When China entered the war, the USSR ceased to sabotage the work of the UN, sent a representative to the Security Council and declared that Russia would make use of the veto to prevent a new offensive. Thus the war finished with stalemate, and the world is still waiting for peace in Korea. The threat of the atomic bomb, although not present at the scene of hostilities, played an important part behind the scenes.

In April 1955 Russia promised to establish atomic piles and cyclotrones in China and train the personnel to take care of them. As Russia had already, in June 1954, finished work on an atom-driven power station, great demonstrations were held in different parts of the People's Republic (130) and the hope of an early development of China's own atomic industry in co-operation with Russia was expressed.

Mao Tse-tung has pointed out that it was the Korean war that caused China to rise, and, while stressing the demand for equality, all the leaders of the People's Republic of China agree that they should keep in close union with their communist comrades in arms. On October 5, 1954, the fifth anniversary of People's Republic, the Russian delegate, Kruschev, exclaimed: 'We are blood brothers!' This was perhaps rather optimistic from the Russian viewpoint, for there are a number of reasons for discontent, and certain Chinese consider that the USSR does not do everything in its power to encourage the Republic's growth of power, and point out that Mao Tse-tung is older than the newcomer, Bulganin, and that China's greater population should be taken into consideration. At the great Asiatic-African Congress in Bandung in Java in April 1955, China, heavily engaged in the Formosa conflict, allowed Chou En-lai to play a more tractable role. The conference, with representatives of twenty-nine countries, was against the manufacture and use of atomic weapons.

Several Russian books dealing with atomic problems have been translated into Chinese, and among Chinese writers on the subject is Dr H. R. Wei, who has been China's representative to the international AEC (131).

The Supreme Organization of the Eastern Powers and the Problem of Atomic Weapons

There is in May 1955 no exact information available as to how the Eastern Powers have organized their supreme leadership. In addition to a network of tracts, which have already been dealt with, there is the actual control which Russia exercises in the satellite states by means of secret organizations in the party, the defence organization and the police. But the aim of the Russian policy is, as shown earlier, to give the appearance of independence so that the policy of infiltration will be made easy in an ever widening sphere of power.

The conference that Russia and her satellites held on December 3, 1954 (the People's Republic of China only sent an observer) was closed with a joint declaration to the effect that combined action for increased military defence should be started if the Western Powers ratified the Paris Treaty regarding the Western European Union. If the treaty were ratified, a joint organization should be created for the supreme command of the Soviet armies and those of the seven European satellites.

If the Western Powers insisted on ratifying the Paris Treaty, a new East Conference was to be held. The Soviet sphere had faith in its strength and inexhaustible resources, and an attack on the Soviet sphere would be re-

THE EASTERN POWERS' VIEW OF THE PROBLEMS

pulsed with great power. To what extent China is willing to take part in a joint supreme command is at present uncertain.

Eastern Germany, Czechoslovakia and Poland have already held conferences on military questions in connection with the rearmament of Eastern Germany. The task of creating a joint command is now in hand.

Inferior to the Western Powers in the production of atomic weapons, and having at present less than half of the Western Power's supply of fissionable materials, the Soviet Union is now straining every muscle to the limit. The American Under-Secretary of State, Bedell Smith, who knows Russia well, said at the end of 1953 that Russia was increasing her military budget, particularly with regard to atomic weapons, and the chairman of the committee for foreign affairs of the French Chamber of Deputies stated recently that Russia increased her production of atomic weapons many times over during 1954! These statements may be exaggerated, but everything indicates that Russia is now making large hydrogen bombs and building large strategic bombers.

It is probable that much less will be learned about the intentions of the Soviet sphere with regard to the use of large and small atomic weapons than what the Western Powers have already announced. We are here touching upon problems which from the point of view of power politics are considered vital by both sides.

The Warsaw Pact concluded in May 1955 deals with mutual assistance and the consolidation of the military forces of the Eastern Powers.

Finally the reader should observe the title of this chapter (p. 67).

Chapter 6

THE TECHNICAL DEVELOPMENT OF ATOMIC WEAPONS

In order to judge what can be done from a political viewpoint about the problem of atomic weapons, we must know the technical characteristics of the different kinds of atomic weapons. It is particularly important to find out whether any line of demarcation can be drawn between large and small atomic weapons. As it is impossible to know in practice, at least for those who are attacked with atomic weapons, whether the object of an action is strategic or tactical, it is impossible to find any distinction there. If a line of demarcation is to be conceivable, it must not lead to a misunderstanding that may be the cause of a great atomic and hydrogen bomb war. It should be observed that what is said below refers to the technical standpoint at the beginning of 1955, and that biological and chemical weapons are dealt with separately in Chapter 10.

The cobalt bomb, which is a hydrogen bomb with a shell of cobalt, is not, so far as is known, being made at present, but any developments in that sphere must be followed carefully. The cobalt bomb, it is said, would produce clouds with a very high degree of radioactivity, many times more dangerous than those produced by a hydrogen or atomic bomb explosion.

Owing to this, it may injure those who drop the bomb, and the clouds may move in unexpected directions, or long contaminate the place, which will prevent both parties from occupying it. But the history of the Japanese suicide pilots may repeat itself, and the danger of a ruthless combatant using cobalt bombs must not be disregarded.

Hydrogen bombs are at present weapons weighing a few tons. But, unlike atomic bombs, they have no critical maximum or minimum values, but can be made of any size. If in spite of that a certain maximum is not exceeded, it is because the effect is quite 'sufficient' in any case, or for convenience of transport. The pressure wave, the heat radiation and the radioactive radiation are so great that it is calculated that a large hydrogen bomb would completely wipe out everything within a radius of 6.5 kilometres, totally demolish most buildings within 8-16 kilometres, cause fires within 11 kilometres, serious pressure damage within 22 kilometres and some damage within a radius of 40 kilometres, if the bomb explodes at a suitable height. The explosive force is about 700 times as great as that of the Hiroshima Bomb, or about the same as that of 14,000,000 tons of TNT, while the Hiroshima bomb had an explosive force of only about 20,000 tons of TNT. The radioactivity of the hydrogen bomb is more dangerous if the explosion takes place at a low altitude. Heat radiation starts from a centre with a temperature of millions of degrees and ignites combustible material at a distance of 9-10 kilometres. The latest hydrogen bombs are said to have an effect 2,000 to 3,000 times greater than that of the Hiroshima bomb!

Heavy atomic bombs now weigh about five tons, and can be carried in bombers of the largest types. Their explosive force is far greater than that of the Hiroshima bomb, or about the same as 500,000 tons of TNT. America is estimated to have at present about 5,000 atomic and hydrogen bombs, and manufactures several hundreds a year. Russia is thought to have less than 1,000 and makes about 100 a year. But the proportion of hydrogen bombs to atomic bombs is very uncertain, and some of the latter have later been converted into hydrogen bombs.

The Hiroshima bomb demolished most of the lightly-built houses up to a distance of 1.6 kilometres from the centre of the explosion, and ignited wood and textiles up to a distance of 1.7 kilometres. And still the number of people killed was very high (cf. p. 48).

The light, or 'tactical', atomic bombs weigh only a few hundred kilogrammes and can be carried in small aeroplanes. Nowadays small, very light hydrogen bombs are being constructed, which make control extremely difficult. As the explosions are relatively small, it is impossible for the great powers to check each other's bomb tests. It should be observed that during a war, bombs with charges approaching the force of that of the Hiroshima bomb may, of course, be considered by the victims to have a much greater effect than such a bomb. The chances of making a mistake will be still greater if several atomic or hydrogen bombs are dropped at the same time. It seems difficult to draw a line of demarcation that is valid in all circumstances, but the problem will be far easier to resolve, if the permitted size limit of such bombs should be kept *as low as is possible* for an international agreement.

The same charges can also be used in atomic shells, atomic rockets, robot weapons and so on.

Atomic artillery consists nowadays of guns of various calibre which, by means of powder charges eject atomic shells charged with light atomic bombs. The heavy 28 cm shells adapted to this use have at present (1954), an effect between 50 and 75 per cent of that of the Hiroshima bomb. It should be impossible, on account of the nature of the bombardment, for anyone attacked with such artillery fire to confuse it with bombs dropped from the air. There

TECHNICAL DEVELOPMENT OF ATOMIC WEAPONS

exist now guns for atomic purposes with a calibre of only 10-12 cm.

The same is the case with short range atomic rockets (atomic torpedoes, atomic mines) fired from artillery pieces on land or sea, and with short range robot weapons (cf. Chapter 11). They can hardly be confused with large atomic weapons.

Larger long range robots are dealt with in Chapter 11.

A very important point is that American bombers have at present a much greater range of action than the Russian.

The consequences of what has been said above will be treated later (Chapter 8), after the question of control has been considered. Defence measures against the different types of 'atomic attack' mentioned above are outside the scope of this work, but it may be mentioned that anti-aircraft shells loaded with atomic charges are a new contribution to air defences.

Chapter 7

POSSIBILITY OF INTERNATIONAL CONTROL

The Author's Conclusions begin with this Chapter

There has been talk of a comprehensive, effective international control of atomic weapons so long that many people have ceased to ask what it really means in practice. From a theoretical point of view it is naturally quite right to fix the goal first, and, when everyone is agreed as to the goal, discuss the ways and means of reaching it. Thus at all the conferences held by the UN the desirability of controlling not only the mines where fissionable material is obtained, but also the transport of the valuable material and its distribution among atomic piles, atomic factories, reactors, experimental stations and laboratories, has been expressed.

The idea has been that no one should be able to hide such material in order to obtain an advantage over other countries by constructing in secret factories atomic weapons that could be used as a threat to other countries, or in a war that had already broken out. All this is good and praiseworthy, but what would this universal control of all fissionable materials, atomic factories and stocks of both small and large atomic weapons really look like?

The author has tried to find out whether any plans have been made in all the UN commissions, but there are no such plans. All that is said is that the whole would be of 'enormous size'. But the investigations made for the compilation of the tables and maps in Appendices 1 and 2 give

POSSIBILITY OF INTERNATIONAL CONTROL

a foundation on which to calculate the probable extent of a maximum control. At the same time it should be borne in mind that as early as 1946, when the international atomic energy commission was formed, the twelve members, all well-known scientists, stated that it was technically possible to organize a system of control, although it was admitted that the treatment of atomic material for peaceful and military use was so similar that it was 'practically impossible' to separate the two uses of fissionable materials. It is, however, a fact that what must be controlled is the amount of fissionable material, but, if that should be impossible, efforts must be made to see that no one makes use of the types of atomic and hydrogen bombs that are forbidden. About 100 inspectors were considered necessary for the supervision of one large mine. As a basis of discussion may be taken the figure—which many experts consider quite inadequate—necessary for the supervision of a larger field of deposits: at least 1,000 inspectors. But let us assume that an average of 100 is sufficient.

In practice a maximum control system would be about as follows:

At present there are in the world about 1,070 more important deposits (see Appendix 2), many of which are so large that they must be assumed to contain several mines, each of which requires separate supervision. It is difficult to give an exact figure, but at least 5,000 mines seems feasible. This gives a staff of 500,000 inspectors for the mines alone, and more and more deposits are being discovered.

The raw material must be transported, under supervision so that nothing is lost on the way, to different kinds of factories and stores (which are often at a great distance), which would require about half the above mentioned figure, that is about 250,000 in the whole organization.

INTERNATIONAL ATOMIC POLICY

At about 100 atomic factories, atomic piles, experimental stations and testing grounds, inspectors must see that no illegal manufactures are carried on. This is considered more difficult than the supervision of mines and about twice as many people, or 200 inspectors will be required for each plant. Laboratories are not included. A staff of about 20,000 would be needed for this work. To make certain that reactors for peaceful ends are not used for the production of war material, such reactors must also be controlled by a smaller staff. As this kind of factory is quite new, we must count on a great increase during the coming decade. This will bring us up to an additional 10,000 persons, in round figures.

It is also considered advisable to control the stocks of existing materials for the manufacture of atomic weapons until, some time in the future, they are destroyed, also under control, of course. This will require a staff of at least 10,000 persons.

All these figures are approximate, but there is no doubt that a maximum control, as it appears from discussions in the United Nations, would require a staff of inspectors, subordinate to the Security Council, the General Assembly and the Atomic Energy Commission, and stationed in most countries of the world, of at least 800,000 strong. In addition, the central organ in the United Nations will require a staff of a size not yet stated.

Over and above the costs of such an organization, it must also be remembered that the great powers are not agreed on the authority which should be vested in the control organization, and who shall have the final decision (without right of veto), and that conflicts caused by different interpretations in various parts of the world will cause misunderstanding and possibly increase tension. One need only think of the difficulties that have arisen

POSSIBILITY OF INTERNATIONAL CONTROL

over the interpretation of the deed of armistice in Korea to understand that control commissions consisting of parties quarrelling among themselves will not be of very great use, and decisions will have to be referred to a higher authority.

Does this mean that the idea of a control intended to counteract the present race for atomic weapons must be given up? Not at all, but only that logic and consideration of what is politically possible make it necessary to restrict control to what really can be controlled, and to carry out this control in a way that does not infringe so seriously in the autonomy of a state that political uneasiness is increased. The system of control should be limited and co-ordinated with President Eisenhower's proposal for an atom bank, to which countries will deliver fissionable material in increasing quantities for purely peaceful use.

More time, therefore, should be devoted at international conferences to what is practically possible, and investigate the possibilities of a simpler and cheaper means of control covering a less comprehensive sphere. To this end the system adopted by the Western European Union, that is, flying visits by groups of inspectors (see p. 60), and that suggested by the author in the *New York Times* and *Revue des deux Mondes*, that the existing military, air and naval attachés, whose duty it is to study defence, including atomic armaments, should be employed. These attachés are already in the centre of the respective countries and are ready to take over the job of inspection without extra pay. The groups of inspectors should naturally also inspect such factories for the production of small atomic and hydrogen weapons as may be suspected of constructing large ones. In this way a system will evolve that will counteract outbreak of war, which is the essential point. When war has broken out, material from small atomic and hydrogen weapons can be used in the manufacture of large ones, but in a great war all international control ceases, and great strain is brought to bear upon international agreements.

But the greatest reduction of supervision can be achieved by relinquishing the supervision of mines, transport and laboratories, which will considerably reduce the need of permanent control in favour of unexpected flying visits by groups of inspectors with permanent authority and guaranteed freedom of movement and entrance to atomic factories, atomic piles, reactor stations, experimental stations and testing grounds. These visits of inspection should not be limited to the places to which the respective governments refer the inspectors, but should be extended to other places where there is reason to suspect that a breach of a treaty may take place or be prepared.

The only way of exercising a practical and satisfactory control seems, on the whole, to be to restrict supervision to the large atomic and hydrogen bombs, which are the least desirable contribution to modern warfare.

If it should be impossible to agree to supervision in the ordinary sense of the word, the only possibility will be to prohibit the use of all hydrogen weapons, both large and small, and rely on an investigation to ascertain whether hydrogen weapons have been used. A scientific body led by the UN must be created for this task. But there will be many political obstacles in the way of such a body as can function in time of war. In this case the problem of punitive measures (sanctions) against those who break a treaty must also be solved.

This idea should, however, be kept in mind in case the other solutions prove to be impracticable (cf. alt. 3-6, p. 131-2).

Chapter 8

LIMITATION OF ALL ATOMIC WEAPONS OR ONLY LARGE ONES?

In a discussion of questions of atomic weapons, not only the technical development now taking place must be taken into consideration, but also the possibilities of control, particularly with regard to cobalt, hydrogen and large atomic bombs. The use of large atomic bombs by the Western Powers is outside the authority of the NATO Commander-in-Chief, but can be authorized by the British and American governments, if possible after consultation with other members of NATO. The probable extent of a retaliation action is a political factor of great importance. It cannot be judged only from the military standpoint.

The top limit of what are considered 'small atomic weapons' is neither fixed nor accepted. The problem has become more complicated recently by the fact that rather small hydrogen bombs, but with very great explosive power, are being constructed. But all the powers seem to be of the opinion that for the smaller bombs the effect of the Hiroshima bomb shall not be exceeded.

The Western powers consider that small atomic weapons are necessary to gain military equality with the Eastern Powers in Europe. But the Western Powers are inclined not to be the first to make use of such atomic weapons, for that could give Russia an excuse for using large atomic weapons against the neighbouring western Europe, which would then be in danger of annihilation.

The Eastern Powers are also manufacturing small atomic weapons of different types.

The standpoint of the Western Powers, according to the meeting of the North Atlantic Council in December 1954, is that small atomic weapons are part of NATO's plans, but that they may not be used until a decision has been made by the governments or by the North Atlantic Council. This shows that the problem of atomic weapons, even with regard to small ones, lies on the border-line between politics and grand military strategy.

It seems possible to consider small atomic weapons as permissible. On the other hand there are reasons for prohibiting small atomic weapons, which now have a very great effect, by fixing a top limit for the explosive power, heat radiation and radioactivity of atomic and hydrogen bombs, much lower than those of the Hiroshima bomb. This limit must be discussed by diplomatic means.

As far as atomic artillery and atomic rockets at short range are concerned, mistakes can hardly be made, while medium-sized, atomic bombs (hydrogen bombs) dropped from the air, and long range robot weapons with atomic charges may lead to mistakes and an increased atomic-bomb war. This is a reason for not using them if mistakes are to be avoided. But small atomic bombs and atomic rockets ought not to be among the weapons prohibited by agreement. It would certainly be much more desirable to prohibit long range robot weapons, even if the problem should be difficult to solve. There is one extremely annoying thing about them: they do not carry proof of the sender's identity.

The conclusion drawn from what has been said above is, therefore, that international negotiations in order to conclude agreements to reduce or stop production of cobalt, large hydrogen and atomic bombs and long-range

LIMITATION OF ALL ATOMIC WEAPONS?

robots (cf. Chapter 11) should be made. Even if their explosive power is not great enough to 'blow up the earth', it must be remembered that an attack with such weapons on the enemy's atomic factories and stocks of atomic weapons may lead to extremely dangerous consequences. If the political situation is favourable, efforts should be made to prohibit unconditionally the use of existing weapons of this type, and stores of such weapons should be destroyed. But there is no hope of this being realized in the present situation. A reasonable control organization, which really can be established, should limit its activities generally to the supervision of these types of weapons, possibly parallel with a financial and numerical limitation, if such can really be created in the future.

But throw overboard the ballast, which a comprehensive maximum control carries with it and which has prevented all results because an unachievable goal has been set! If a restricted task can be carried through successfully, which in itself may be difficult enough, the more complicated problems may be solved gradually when the situation improves.

But let us stop talking about strategic and tactical atomic weapons, and talk about large and small instead!

Chapter 9

ABSOLUTE OR CONDITIONAL PROHIBITION OF THE USE OF ATOMIC WEAPONS?

A stumbling-block, which still exists between East and West, is that Russia, according to Malenkov's announcement at the turn of the year 1954-55, still maintained that if with regard to the limitation of atomic weapons it was agreed on principle to prohibit their use, this prohibition should be unconditional, that is to say, no exceptions should be made. Thus a state that was attacked would not be allowed to use such weapons in its defence.

The Western Powers hold the opinion that the use of the weapons should be allowed against states that had ignored the prohibition, and also in defence against attack, even with conventional, military armaments. This standpoint is calculated to deter states from beginning wars of aggression. During the negotiations in London during the summer of 1954, the Western Powers appended the proposal that a third state (e.g. a member of NATO) should have the right, as a punitive measure, to help an attacked state with the use of atomic weapons—an extension that was bitterly opposed by Russia. The Western Powers were naturally of the opinion that an unconditional prohibition of atomic weapons would encourage Russia to begin new aggressions in more or less disguised forms, a possibility that cannot be ignored.

Up to now, no mention of different types of atomic weapons has been made at all these negotiations, but they

ABSOLUTE OR CONDITIONAL PROHIBITION?

have all been treated alike. But unless we are willing to be satisfied when no results are achieved, and the race for atomic weapons is intensified, would it not be reasonable to attempt to solve the most dangerous problem first, and let the less dangerous wait? If it is agreed to distinguish between large and small atomic weapons, which seems to be the only feasible way with regard to control, what will then be the position of the question of prohibition of use?

There seem to be several possible solutions, but the one that most actively contributes to the preservation of peace, that is to say, counteracts aggression, should be sought. Here are my proposals:

(1) All means should be allowed, both large (as long as they last) and small atomic weapons, against a state that ignores the prohibition of the use of atomic weapons and begins using them.

(2) Against a state that begins a war of aggression, but only with conventional arms, the defence should be allowed to use small atomic weapons immediately; it will be in the interest of the defender not to use such weapons as would lead the aggressor to believe that large atomic or hydrogen bombs have been used. This will counteract aggression.

(3) The right of a third state to come to the help of a state that has been attacked should be calculated so that if the aggressor uses forbidden atomic weapons, all means should be allowed, but if only conventional weapons have been used, the help should comprise only small atomic weapons, which cannot be confused with large ones, but not the large weapons themselves.

(4) If a state claims falsely that the small atomic weapons used were large ones, and on these grounds threatens to use, or uses large atomic weapons, it may be

subject to retaliation of the same kind, in accordance with (1) above.

These proposals may of course be modified, but they seem to allow of an escape from the dead-end 'unconditional or conditional prohibition of use'. They should be able to count on the support of all who really wish to preserve peace, and the international discussions of the proposals should show where the real friends of peace are to be found in the world. The proposals were drawn up before the USA, in January 1955, announced that a retaliation plan had been evolved there to double the damage for those who began a war of aggression (Plan Two-X). This plan is based on severe reprisals, and cannot be used as the basis of an international agreement. We are here concerned with two different things; in one case the attempt to come to a solution by means of agreements that remove the dissonance between the unconditional and the conditional prohibition, and in the other case a principle which the USA eventually will recommend her allies to accept.

After a discussion of the above proposals it should be easier to come to an agreement with regard to conditional prohibition.

Chapter 10

BIOLOGICAL AND CHEMICAL WEAPONS

In the designation ABC weapons, B indicates biological or bacteriological weapons and C chemical weapons. Spread over a country by the 'fifth column', dropped from the air or carried by robot weapons they constitute a great danger, the significance of which can hardly be distinguished by the terms 'large' and 'small'. Epidemic diseases, borne by water, air or in food, cannot be calculated in advance, nor can their effect on the population or the fighting forces. The same is the case with so-called military gases.

The use of poison gas was prohibited before 1914, but that did not prevent their being used extensively during the years 1914-18. Nerve gases, mustard gas and hydrocyanic acid gas have been spread from the air by bombs and by direct spreading from aeroplanes. But even artillery, shell throwers and rocket weapons may be used. Here, however, the problem must be restricted to its political, not technical, aspects.

The fact that gas was not used in the Second World War (although Japan had specially trained forces for such warfare) nor in the Korean war is no guarantee that the events of 1916-18 will not be repeated with a greater degree of intensity due to the rate of development. Thus the USA, in a report to the United Nations in 1946, stated that measures taken by the Western Powers were aimed at reducing the effect of a gas war and building up an organization for *reprisals* against those who began biological or chemical warfare. This is also the basis of the work in most countries where questions of biological warfare, different kinds of gas or other chemical weapons are being dealt with. Radiological weapons have already been mentioned. Extensive preparation has been carried out in many countries, and is being extended in keeping with changes in the situation.

The American Atomic Energy Commission has pointed out several times in its reports the importance of keeping the safety services in a state of constant vigilance, not only during atomic bomb tests, but at times of political tension, to be on the watch for radioactive particles from atomic clouds and the intentional spreading of gas. Chains of safety services have been established in many states, for this is a dangerous form of injury, and great humanitarian values are at stake.

Everyone is agreed that some kind of control of this type of warfare must be included in a future international agreement. The Geneva Convention of 1925 must be brought up to date and extended. But as in its ratification instrument, there must be included the reservation that such weapons may be used against a state that ignores the prohibition. It is obvious that this will create a deterrent, and the principle that was so effective during the Second World War, respect for reprisals or sanctions, will be followed. If that line is followed, equality in B and C weapons as well as A weapons will be kept, in the same way as is described in Chapter 9. Although it is impossible to distinguish between large and small BC weapons, it is clear that those making use of them expose themselves to great risks, also from the states that come to the help of a victim of aggression. This is appropriate in the interests of peace and humanity.

It is extremely desirable that control is extended to

BIOLOGICAL AND CHEMICAL WEAPONS

cover B and C weapons, but it is not essential if their control proves too complicated and for that reason cannot be accepted. Efforts should be made, however, to organize control, which could be made easier by an agreement that the manufacture of all such biological and chemical weapons shall be centralized. In that case, control would be much more feasible.

Every country should protect itself by extending its customs control to prevent biological and chemical weapons—and, of course, atomic and hydrogen bombs—being smuggled in for sabotage. Safety services must be greatly extended.

Chapter 11

ROBOT WEAPONS

The problem of robot weapons was dealt with in Chapter 8 for the sake of coherence, but the various types of robot weapons require some explanation. Unlike rocket weapons, which are propelled by liquid fuel and the like, robot weapons are driven by jet engines. The warhead varies in size in accordance with the purpose of the robot.

There is an undoubted tendency to load large, long-range robots of types V1, V2 and others with warheads similar to atomic and hydrogen bombs with an effect at the same level as that of the Hiroshima bomb. The robots with a very high path may easily be confused with large atomic bombs dropped from the air, and even a radar system may fail to distinguish between them. In view of their range and effect, it is impossible to classify them as 'small weapons'. They are typical, long-range weapons, like atomic and hydrogen bombs carried by air. It may be objected that their explosive force can be lower than that of the Hiroshima bomb, but charged with a hydrogen bomb their effect can be great, even with a smaller charge.

It seems logical, therefore, to assign long-range robots with a range of, for instance, over 150-250 kilometres* to the same class as the large atomic weapons, and by agreement treat them in the same way. That is, production shall be stopped and their use regulated according to Chapter 9, and their destruction in the future shall be considered in connection with the large atomic weapons.

*Only negotiations can show which figure is most suitable.

ROBOT WEAPONS

There will probably be opposition from the side of the Soviet, for much work has been done there, and much money invested in long-range robot weapons, but the USA has got at least as far, and Western Europe has now also such robots.

On the other hand, it seems quite logical to assign ground robots, fighter robots, attack robots, sea robots and coast robots, anti-tank robots and anti-aircraft robots and so on with a range of less than 150-250 kilometres to the same class as short-range rockets, that is to say, as small atomic weapons, even if they are loaded with small atomic or hydrogen bombs, and treat them in accordance with those weapons (see Chapter 9).

All robot weapons, like other weapons, loaded with biological, chemical or radiological mediums should, in view of what has been said in Chapter 10, be completely prohibited. Both East and West have several hundreds of kilogrammes of radiological substance (atomic ash) each.

Long-range robots of trans-oceanic range threaten to create defence problems that will be very difficult to solve for all countries, and contribute largely to uncertainty and anxiety in the world.

Chapter 12

CONNECTION BETWEEN ABC WEAPONS AND CONVENTIONAL ARMAMENTS

The historical-political investigation has shown that there is an intimate connection between ABC weapons and other armaments, so that the possession of atomic weapons may partly compensate for a shortage of other weapons. But this cannot be carried too far. A country with a shortage of conventional armaments will cut a poor figure if attacked, unless an atomic war begins, for the enemy will have several reasons for avoiding an atomic war. It must also be borne in mind that a state with atomic bombs attacking another state which has no atomic bombs, has a great military advantage. This may encourage wars of aggression against countries without atomic weapons.

We have observed from conference discussions that attempts have sometimes been made to work out coefficients, so that a certain number of atomic bombs should be counted as equal to a certain number of army divisions and the like. But all such attempts have been unsuccessful, for the problem cannot be solved, as the value of different kinds of armaments varies with the military situation, political and strategical circumstances and the use that can be made of atomic weapons. The equation has too many unknown quantities to allow of a solution or simplification.

Nor can an increase of conventional armaments com-

ABC WEAPONS AND CONVENTIONAL ARMAMENTS

pensate for a lack of atomic weapons. When the necessary means of defence are being calculated for a country, the likelihood or possibility of being attacked with atomic weapons must influence not only the budget and organization, but also the distribution of the fighting forces and their grouping.

If it is assumed—which really is the case—that all the great powers are agreed on the prohibition of B and C weapons (although the risk that they may be used will probably necessitate a certain state of preparation in case of this danger), only H and A weapons remain. If any result is to be arrived at with regard to these, it is useless to waste time on the theoretically correct thought that it would have been better if they had never been invented or that they could all disappear. As development makes such a solution impossible, the only thing that remains is to ignore the small atomic weapons, the manufacture of which can in any case never be effectively controlled, and include them in conventional armaments.

On the other hand negotiations for the limitation of large atomic weapons should be taken up again. The prohibition of only hydrogen and cobalt bombs might be considered, for these have a far greater effect than ordinary atomic bombs. But the large atomic bombs, the effect of which is as great as, or greater than that of the Hiroshima bomb, are also terrible weapons, more suitable for mass destruction of densely populated areas than in a struggle for a certain definite military objective. This gives the large atomic weapons and long-range robots a special position, which is the decisive factor in the inhumanity of modern warfare.

If, however, we ignore the connection between small atomic weapons and conventional armaments, which is more a military than a political problem, the relationship of large atomic weapons to conventional armaments remains a political-military question of the greatest significance.

The race for large atomic weapons is now extremely keen, and only those with a very clear superiority in this respect can view the future with a feeling of security. It is generally agreed nowadays, however, that a quantitative superiority does not ensure true security. For this so-called security is disturbed by the risk that a state that is inferior in atomic weapons but with unscrupulous leaders, may, by means of coup, gain superiority, which can change the course of the history of the world. Atomic weapons, unfortunately, give enormous significance to a surprise attack. To come to some result with regard to the restriction of large atomic weapons is perhaps the greatest political problem facing the world today. But the solution must not imply that the true democratic, cultural states, on which stability in the world depends, are to be weakened.

All international conference activities during the past decade show that if the solution of the problem of atomic weapons is delayed by being made too comprehensive and complicated, no progress can be made in the question of military armaments. It is the race for atomic arms that causes a natural feeling of alarm in all countries and this in its turn increases anxiety and leads to demands for increased defence measures all round. This is the psychological heart of the matter.

Conventional armaments have the advantage of being suitable for defence, even if they can be used in a war of aggression. But the weapons that ought to be designated 'large atomic weapons' are mainly intended as weapons of attack, which augments the anxiety they cause. It must be admitted, however, that the large atomic weapons have the purpose of deterring a hostile state from beginning a war of aggression. But if this effect can be obtained with less frightful means, that is, with the help of forces armed with atomic weapons of a more limited effect, such as smaller atomic weapons, it would be an advantage.

And if an agreement could be reached for the gradual restriction of the large atomic weapons, there is no doubt at all that a more favourable situation would be created for the limitation of other kinds of armaments, too.

The question will be decided according to what degree the political leaders in the world consider, with due regard to their responsibility for the welfare of nations and humanity, they can take the risk of reducing their so-called 'margin of security'. If such a margin can be assured by other means than the most inflammatory, it will also be to the advantage of the leading nations.

Chapter 13

ATOMIC ENERGY IN PEACE AND WAR

All well-informed people are agreed that atomic power will play a very important part in the lives of all human beings in the immediate future. It may be compared with electricity and the application of electric energy all over the world. It provides inexhaustible resources for the production of power after the world's supply of fuel has been exhausted, or a country has exploited all other sources of power. The use of atomic energy in medicine by means of isotopes is increasing at an enormous speed. New discoveries are expected in several spheres, and nuclear reactions will be effected in new and cheaper ways than those now known.

New possibilities will be opened up for great powers that have built up an atomic industry on a large scale, to strengthen their positions in the world, but also to help countries less favoured from the point of view of power to utilize atomic energy in peaceful ways, or to defend their independence. The leading powers have in atomic energy a new source of wealth, influence and the possibility to help others. The most important thing for humanity is that an increased proportion of the newly-created atomic energy is used to foster peaceful progress in the world. In this, Eisenhower's proposal for an atom bank is the obvious means. The possibility of denaturing fissionable material and thus making it useless for atomic bombs without a long, complicated and expensive process, facilitates the creation of an international pool. The USA has taken the lead, but up to January 1955 the Soviet has not shown any tendency to join, but tried to form an 'Eastern Pool', with the satellite states and the peoples of Asia. The final result of the present difference of opinion cannot be judged in advance.

Reactors are now being constructed in the USA for both large and medium-sized plants, and on quite new principles. A great increase in atomic industry for peaceful ends can be expected all over the world, encouraged by support from both America and Russia. In many places the economic tug-of-war between the leading powers can already be detected, reminiscent of that which characterized the struggle for the world's oilwells earlier. This is especially the case in countries which do not belong to either one side or the other, where commercial contracts for the import of uranium ore and the like are a very important factor. The map (Appendix 3) shows that certain parts of South America, South Africa, India and Indonesia are extremely important from the point of view of raw materials. As far as the USA is concerned, the new deposits in Canada provide a very valuable addition. But the application of atomic energy to peaceful ends has an economic-commercial aspect that will be very important in the future.

A careful study of the uranium deposits of the Soviet shows that the Soviet's policy is to help China, Poland, Czechoslovakia, Rumania and Eastern Germany generously with fissionable material, atomic piles and scientific and industrial help for the peaceful use of atomic energy. It is the intention to make use of the experience gained in Russia, and to remove natural obstacles, change the courses of rivers and construct canals through the country which is to be rebuilt, in accordance with Stalin's favourite theory. But at the same time, the Soviet is chary of giving her satellites and allies the possibilities of making large atomic weapons. For their dependence upon Russia is a very important part of Soviet policy, besides which it will be easier to retain the lead in the Eastern Powers if Russia alone has the means of using serious threats. It should be observed that atomic weapons have given Russia increased possibilities of following her traditional policy of infiltration, with a carefully thought out combination of generous promises and threats.

A rapidly increasing atomic legislation has followed in the wake of the utilization of atomic energy for peaceful ends, as has already been mentioned, in leading nations and wherever new problems crop up. Great international tasks have arisen to advance the peaceful use of atomic energy, which have already had repercussions in respect to conferences. In November 1954 questions of atomic energy were treated by the United Nations. The Western Powers proposed that an International Atomic Energy Agency should be created to collaborate with the United Nations organization, and that the UN should convene a technical conference at Geneva (133). The General Assembly confirmed this (134). The Secretary-General is to set up a conference organization with the help of the representatives of certain states (135), and means were granted (136). The Soviet will also take part in this conference. The year 1955 will be rich in events touching upon atomic problems. The great international conference which started at Geneva on August 8 will be of immense importance.

The later events of the year 1955 are certainly known by the actual newspaper-press.

Chapter 14

SUMMARY

A profound study of questions of atomic weapons gives even those who work with such problems the opportunity of critical scrutiny. The author started with the theory that all atomic weapons, both large and small, should be controlled. But a careful study of the practical possibility of control, among other things, has *made a change in this standpoint inevitable*. It appeared essential to see the problem on a large scale, and see it from *a new and more rational angle*. Knowledge is not enough, we must also show a sense of reality. We are, perhaps, one illusion poorer with regard to the idea of collective security in the whole world, and are compelled to fall back on a balance of power, which, it is hoped, will make it possible to avoid war. The author's conclusions are expressed in the following nineteen points.

We have entered upon a new age, the atomic age, the outlines of which can be discerned, but which in any case compels us to revise many of our deep-rooted notions. We must realize that developments in atomic science move towards goals that are still unknown to us. Now it is the nucleus that is the main subject of study, together with the so-called mesons which hold the protons and neutrons of the nucleus together. Gigantic accelerators are being built for the mass production of different kinds of mesons (e.g. the European laboratory for nuclear research at Geneva). By studying radioactivity attempts are being made to investigate the structure of the nucleus. No one knows yet where that will lead.

INTERNATIONAL ATOMIC POLICY

But it is certain that the conference mentality that has allowed ten years of discussion of the prohibition of atomic weapons while the leading powers have been eagerly, and without any consideration of costs, engaged in a wild race for armaments, has not done any good. Instead of theoretical propaganda, intended to reassure people in all countries with the feeling that something positive is being done, we must demand practical realism, which does not embellish, but which is more valuable. We cannot sit with our arms folded and hope that perhaps 'the march of science will make war impossible'. We must try to help peaceful development on the right path.

It is only by stages that mankind has realized what enormous forces we are dealing with, and to tame the forces of nature is often beyond the power of human beings. This error of judgment has caused international conferences to set a goal that they had not the power to reach. These conferences were made necessary by public opinion after a world war, while the political situation, as shown in Chapters 2-5, was often very unfavourable. In particular the situation in Eastern Europe, the struggle over the future of Germany and the Korean war were great obstacles in the way of a relaxation of political tension. In fact, it is difficult to imagine a less favourable situation.

Historically and politically it is quite clear how great an influence the development of atomic weapons has been. In particular the possibility that Germany, after the first splitting of the uranium atom there in 1938, would have been first with the atomic bomb, produced by the mighty German armaments industry, gives food for thought. How would the war have ended if unscrupulous German leaders had had atomic weapons at their disposal instead of the non-decisive V1 and V2 weapons?

SUMMARY

What would the end of the war, and the post-war years have been like if the USA had not made her gigantic efforts in time, and the Soviet had been the first with the large atomic bomb? What power it would have given to Stalin's words in a war-worn Europe! And how would the Russian blockade of Berlin (1948-49) have finished if the Soviet alone had had the atomic bomb?

As far as the hydrogen bomb was concerned, the Soviet was before America in some respects, but if the USA had not at the last moment speeded up her production of hydrogen bombs and, thanks to her well-developed atomic industry, caught up with and passed the Soviet, what would the balance of power been then, in spite of the creation of the North Atlantic Treaty Organization and its consolidation? Would the USA have supported Western Europe so generously?

The uranium fever of 1946-55 has doubled the known deposits many times over, as shown in Appendix 2 and the map (Appendix 3). Fissionable material increases by leaps and bounds, and atomic scientists expect an extension of nuclear reaction that will cause greater difficulties for international control. It is not possible to build up a control organization that would control effectively the production of fissionable material in mines all over the world, or see that material is not 'lost in transit' between, say, South Africa and the USA, or between the mines in northern Siberia and the atomic centres of the Soviet. A maximum control, such as put forward by the United Nations, would be carried on permanently with regard not only to all atomic factories, experimental stations, testing grounds and possibly laboratories but also—as proposed by the Soviet—to places where reactors are in operation for peaceful ends, to see that atomic weapons were not made there instead. Many experts consider that up to

1,000,000 people would be hardly sufficient for all these duties, besides which there must in any case be a central organization of considerable size at the UN or in collaboration with the UN. To this can be added that as long as the existing mistrust remains in the world it is open to question whether such an enormous control organization would really be of any value in view of the episodes that would surely take place if detailed control with great authority were resorted to. But if control is restricted to a suitable minimum control of only the most dangerous weapons, it is quite possible that it could be organized.

If it is asked which weapons are most inhuman and most likely to cause injury to non-combatants, the answer must be the large hydrogen (H) and atomic (A) weapons (including long-range robots) and biological (B) and chemical (C) weapons, which latter are by no means easy to control. Many scientists are inclined to rank both C and perhaps B weapons before A weapons. If the smaller atomic weapons are called 'a-weapons' and the smaller hydrogen weapons 'h-weapons' the order will probably be HABCha.

As the supervision of h- and a-weapons will probably require the organization of a very dense net of control stations, it will be impossible to realize in practice, besides which, these weapons are already included in the ordinary armaments of both East and West.

The abandonment of the control of a-weapons, and possibly h-weapons, will be more than compensated for by the fact that more time and opportunity will be gained for the control of the most dangerous and inhuman weapons, which is by far most important. And a large number of small hydrogen or atomic weapons cannot cause such catastrophes as H and A weapons may lead to.

Investigations to find a solution favourable for humanity

SUMMARY

and acceptable politically, by putting aside less important problems, show that it is necessary to cut a 'golden section' through the tangle of limitations, prohibitions and questions of control. The section must be made so that practical results are attained, and it is—in order to reach agreement—quite necessary to balance the measures in such a way as to ensure that the result will be a *uniform limitation of the possibility of offence* on both sides, and a *uniform and impartial exposure of secrets* by both East and West.

Let us confine our efforts to the most dangerous HABC weapons, and ignore the prohibition of a-weapons and possibly h-weapons, for which a maximum explosive power—much lower than that of the Hiroshima bomb—heat radiation and radioactivity must be fixed by agreement!

Drop the idea of permanent control of mines, supervision of the transport of enormous quantities of material, experimental stations, testing grounds, laboratories and reactors for peaceful ends, for it cannot be realized. Retain the control of atomic factories where HABC weapons (possibly h-weapons and long-range robots) are made, and model the control organization on that of the Western European Union, with a minimum control system which gives the right to make flying inspections at other places than those reported by the respective states (i.e. at experimental stations and the like). Facilitate the organization by making use of the foreign military attachés stationed in the respective countries, and appoint atomic attachés. Disputes must be referred to a central organization under the United Nations, where they will be settled without right of veto.

The aim of a conference or of international negotiations on questions of atomic weapons ought to be to create an agreement on quite different principles than those hitherto applied, and aim, as is shown in Chapter 9, at eliminating the antagonism between conditional and unconditional prohibition. If that fails, a solution must be sought via conditional prohibition. A change has taken place in the Soviet's demand for unconditional prohibition which indicates that there is a possibility that Russia is not so determined as formerly.

The results first aimed at in a gradual limitation should be chiefly concerned with the production of HA weapons and later with their prohibition, the prohibition of B and C weapons, as proposed in Chapter 10, and a timetable for the relationship between the limitation of HABC weapons and that of conventional armaments.

The reader will have observed that this proposal by no means prevents the great powers from resorting to the 'language of force' in the interests of peace. The fact that the production of HA weapons stops, but the existing stocks are kept for the time being, and that the prohibition of their use is only conditional, makes them a powerful deterrent against aggression, for the Western Powers from the East, for the Eastern Powers from the West. In addition, the superiority of the Western Powers as regards small atomic weapons is so great that they create a state of approximate equilibrium in the balance of power. The proposal, therefore, takes into consideration the only foundation on which an agreement can be based, that is, *the retention of the present balance of power*. In this way the Western Powers, the bearers of culture, will not be compelled to give up their essential margin of security, for the forbidden weapons may be used against aggression. A relaxation of tension cannot be achieved by compelling a reduction in armaments, but it *ought* to be possible to agree to a limitation of the most dangerous HABC weapons, if this limitation were equally advantageous for both parties.

SUMMARY

The development of atomic energy in the interests of peace should be encouraged in every possible way, not only because it supplies the world with a new and necessary source of power, but also because its use in the interests of peace will influence the great powers to satisfy the demands of peace at the expense of those of war, which tend to increase tension in the world, and which have created one of humanity's greatest problems. Help to technically underdeveloped countries to use atomic power for peaceful ends is one of the great tasks of certain of the great powers.

There are naturally always objections to proposed solutions of all great problems, and improvements can no doubt be made in the system. But the best kind of criticism is to propose something better! The solution suggested above seems in the present situation to be the most logical goal for the efforts made during the immediate future. Eleven alternative solutions have been examined by the author and are to be found on pages 131-2, and by seeking after truth the advantages and disadvantages of the different alternatives have been revealed.

It does not follow that the proposed method can be easily realized immediately. A reduction of armaments is a goal that is still far distant, and the way to it goes via a limitation of the most potent weapons of mass destruction. The suggestion that conventional armaments should be limited first, and then atomic weapons will, according to all experience, not lead to any results at international conferences.

Humanity's instinct for self-preservation should be respected. Efforts should be made to find a method that is practical and that will lead to a relaxation of tension by stages, in the true interests of humanity and peace, before development during the next few years aggravates the situation with regard to questions of atomic weapons. The obstinate resistance of human beings to thinking on a grand scale must be broken down by enlightened men and women devoting themselves to bringing about a spiritual nuclear fission that will put a stop to the urge to create more and more devastating, and for the existence of humanity risky means of warfare for use in the struggle of the people of the world about how to achieve greater happiness! If this nuclear fission can begin a chain reaction that spreads in wider and wider circles, there is a chance that leading statesmen will be able to find their way through the alternative solutions towards the middle of the table. We are compelled to seek a solution which, for the sake of humanity, *must be found!*

SUMMARY

PLAN FOR THE ABOLITION BY STAGES OF CERTAIN WEAPONS

Altern-ative	Nature of the solution	Alternative's symbol
1.	The limitation of the production of *only large hydrogen bombs* (H-bombs, possibly also cobalt bombs) to a certain percentage of the annual production of fissionable material, in collaboration with an international atomic bank which encourages the peaceful use of atomic energy and restricts extensive experiments with bombs.	H%
2.	As 1, but applicable to both *large H-bombs* and *A-bombs*	HA%
3.	Cessation of production of *only large H-bombs* (and possibly h-bombs) above a certain size, which can be gradually reduced, and *conditional prohibition* of all such weapons as may be in existence.	H/con.
4.	Cessation of production of *large H- and A-bombs* under control, and the conditional prohibition of their use. Can be made more strict by including h-bombs.	HA/con.
5.	Cessation of production, under control, of H, A (h?) and long-range robots (R) with charges of H and A, and conditional prohibition of their use, etc.	HAR/con.

Alternative	Nature of the solution	Alternative's symbol
6.	Cessation of production, under control, of H, A (h?) and R loaded with H, A, h and a, and B and C weapons, and conditional prohibition of their use, etc.	HARBC/con.
7.	Cessation of production of H, A, R, B and C weapons, and h and a weapons, under control of an immense control organization, and conditional prohibition of their use, etc.	HARBCha/con.
8.	One of the above alternatives with *unconditional* prohibition (gives seven secondary alternatives).	1-7 uncon.
9.	Destruction of stocks of H, A, R, B, C and unconditional prohibition with a large control organization (with a time limit?)	HARBC/uncon. destruction.
10.	Destruction of stocks of H, A, R, B, C and of h-bombs with very large control organization and unconditional prohibition	HARBCh/uncon. destruction.
11.	As 10, but including all small atomic weapons (h, a-bombs, weapons with such charges and small robots and rockets /r/).	HARBChar/uncon. destruction.

Conclusion: An examination has shown that Alternative 6 is what should be realized in the first place, and after that Alternatives 5, 4 and 3. Alternatives 1-2 are insufficient to lead to relaxation, Alternatives 7-11 cannot be realized in the reasonably near future.

APPENDIX 1

Sources

The following sources have been of great value:
1. United Nations, An International Bibliography on Atomic Energy, Vol. 1, Political, Economic and Social Aspects, New York 1949, 45 pages, important; indicates 854 sources.
   ——Supplement No. 1, 1950, 22 pages, 274 sources.
   ——Supplement No. 2, 1953, 31 pages, 394 sources.
2. United Nations, An International Bibliography on Atomic Energy, Vol. 2, Scientific Aspects, New York 1951. Also contains facts about history and policy. 500 pages, important.
   ——Supplement No. 1, 1952, 150 pages.
   ——Supplement No. 2, 1953, 160 pages.
   With supplements 40,000 sources.
3. A. Einstein: Relativity; the Special and the General Theory, 1905. New edition 1931. A. Einstein and N. Rosen: The particle problem in the general theory of relativity, *Phys. Review*, New York 1935. Nils Bohr: Speech in Stockholm, December 1922 (Nobel Prize Speech). Books on nuclear physics, especially D. Dietz: Atomic Science, Bombs and Power, New York 1954, 315 pages, gives a popular description of the fundamentals of nuclear science.
4. H. D. Smyth. A General Account of the Development of Methods of using Atomic Energy for Military Purposes, Princeton 1954; important.
5. Agreed declaration by the President of the United States, the Prime Minister of the United Kingdom and the Prime Minister of Canada, Washington, November 15, 1954, and Soviet-Anglo-American Communiqué, Moscow, Conference December 27, 1945.
6. United Nations, Official Documents, General Assembly January 10—February 14, 1946, and Security Council, Official Records July 10, 1946.
7. United Nations Atomic Energy Commission. First Report, December 31, 1946, 100 pages, important (accepted by ten delegates. Russia and Poland refrained from voting).
8. United Nations, Scientific and Technical Aspects of the Control of Atomic Energy, 1946.

9. H. D. Smyth (cf. 4) and Revs. Modern Phys. 1945.
10. D. E. Lilienthal and others: First Report of the US Atomic Energy Commission, *Science*, 1947.
11. The following books contain interesting, supplementary information:
    (a) The International Control of Atomic Energy, Scientific Information, October 1946, 195 pages.
    (b) The International Control of Atomic Energy, Scientific Information, December 1946, 30 pages.
    (c) The Control of Atomic Energy, United Nations Information Section, New York 1946.
12. United Nations, Official Documents, General Assembly, 1947, and Security Council, Official Records, February 13 and March 10, 1947.
13. B. M. Baruch: Scientific Information to the United Nations Atomic Energy Commission, June 1946, and Statement on Atomic Energy, *New York Times*, October 3, 1946.
14. United Nations Atomic Energy Commission, Second Report, September 11, 1947, with majority and minority proposals and delegates' speeches, 262 pages (accepted by ten delegates. Russia and Poland refrained from voting).
15. United Nations Atomic Energy Commission, Third Report, May 17, 1948, with proposals and delegates' speeches, 78 pages, important.
16. United Nations, Official Documents, General Assembly 1948, and Security Council, Official Records, June 22, 1948.
17. United Nations, Proposals and Recommendations of Atomic Energy Commission, 1948. Gives a survey of the work 1946-48, and accounts of the Soviet proposal, 120 pages. Among many pamphlets may be mentioned 'Exposition sur l'Energie Atomique', Paris 1949.
18. Terminological Calendar of Expressions concerning Atomic Energy, in English, French (énergie atomique), Russian (atomnaja energija), Spanish (energía atómica) and Chinese.
19. Andrew Morton: Collective Security, United Nations, 1952, 250 pages, deals with conditions to the end of 1951, and is rather brief on the subject of atomic weapons.
20. See Chapters 4 and 5.
21. Swedish Minister of Foreign Affairs, Ö. Undén, General Assembly, September 26, 1950, and protocols from the Swedish Parliament.

APPENDIX I

22. United Nations, Annual Report of Secretary General, July 1, 1951—June 30, 1952.
23. E. Biörklund: The limitation of armaments of the Great Powers, *World Horizon*, Göteborg, January and February, 1953.
24. United Nations Disarmament Commission, February—December 1952, 700 pages, important.
25. United Nations, Annual Report of Secretary General, July 1, 1952—June 30, 1953.
26. E. Biörklund: The new Russian regime, *Svensk Tidskrift* No. 9, 1953.
27. E. Biörklund: Decrease of tension step by step, *Svenska Dagbladet*, December 13, 1953.
28. United Nations, General Assembly, 1953, and Annual Report of Secretary General July 1, 1953—June 30, 1954.
29. Major Problems of United States Foreign Policy, New York 1954.
30. United Nations Disarmament Commission, New York 1954 and Disarmament Subcommittee, London 1954.

---

31. B. M. Baruch, Department of State Publication, 2661, 2702, 3161, and *New York Times*, October 3, 1946.
32. Committee on Atomic Energy, Department of State Publication, 2498, 1946.
33. International Conciliation, New York, Nos. 416, 423 and 430.
34. A. W. Dulles: *Foreign Affairs*, New York, January 1947.
35. Masters, Way and others: One World or None. McGraw-Hill Publishing Co., New York, 1946.
36. (a) H. W. Baldwin: Great Mistakes of the War. New York, 1950.
    (b) E. M. Zacharias: We did not need to drop the A-bomb. *Look*, New York, May 23 and June 6, 1950.
37. Operation Crossroads, New York 1946, 222 pages illustrations for the report; important.
    Official Report: Bombs at Bikini. New York 1947, 212 pages, important.
38. H. W. Baldwin: The Price of Power. New York, 1948.
39. Harry Truman: The Department of State Bulletin, USA, October, 1949.
40. Harry Truman: The Department of State Bulletin, USA, January 31, 1950.
41. 'Atom Bomb', in *Air Affairs*, Washington, April 1950.

42. E. Rabinovitj: Minutes to Midnight, Chicago, April 1950.
43. A. Einstein, Preface to book: America, Russia and the Bomb, Washington, June 1950.
44. (a) US Congress. Joint Committee on Atomic Energy, 81st Congress, 2nd Session, March 1950, and US Department of Defense and US Atomic Energy Commission, Washington, June 1950.
    (b) J. R. Oppenheimer: Science and the Common Understanding, 1953, and
    (c) N. Bohr: Atomic Theory and the Nature, 1934; Discussions with Einstein, 1949.
45. US Congress, Joint Committee on Atomic Energy, Washington, November 1952, contains a survey of the laws and regulations up to 1952.
46. (a) J. R. Shepley-Cl. Blair: The Hydrogen Bomb. New York, 1954, interesting, but perhaps not reliable.
    (b) B. Brodie: The atom bomb as policy maker, *Foreign Affairs*, October 1948.
    (c) M. Evans: The Secret War for the A-bomb. Chicago, 1953, contains much about espionage in the USA, 1945-53.
47. Major Activities in the Atomic Energy Programmes, January-December 1953, 249 pages; interesting, particularly with regard to organization.
48. Semi-annual Report of the Atomic Energy Commission, 1953, which contains information about the organization of the commission and gives a lot of facts about the USA, of which no comparison could be imagined in Russian literature.
49. H. W. Baldwin, *New York Times*, 1954.
    G. Dean: Report on the Atom. New York, 1953, very important.
    J. Burnham: Containment or Liberation. New York, 1953.
    B. Brodie: Nuclear Weapons, *Foreign Affairs*, January 1954.
50. D. Eisenhower: The Department of State Bulletin, December 1953.
51. Major Activities in the Atomic Energy Programmes, January-July 1954; 137 pages, important.
52. E. Biörklund: Study on America's view of the question of nuclear weapons.
53. American articles in different periodicals at the end of 1954, and Gordon Dean: Report on the Atom.
54. Final Act of the Nine-Power Conference, London, September 28—October 3, 1954, H.M. Stationery Office, London. 22

APPENDIX I

pages, important. The resistance of France to the EDC proposal is discussed in Jules Moch's work: Alerte! Paris, 1954.
55. Documents agreed on by the Conference of Ministers held in Paris, October 20-23, 1953. HM Stationery Office, London. 60 pages, very important.
56. Parliamentary Debates, *Hansard*, London, 1948-55.
57. (a) Sir G. Thomson, articles 1892-1930.
    (b) M. L. Oliphant: Control of Atomic Energy, London, 1946, and Atomic Age 1949.
    (c) B. Russell: The Atomic Bomb and the Prevention of War. Chicago, 1946.
    New Hopes for a Changing World, George Allen & Unwin, London, 1952.
    Nightmares of Prominent Persons. John Lane, The Bodley Head, London, 1954.
    (d) Lord Hankey: International Control. London, 1947.
    The Atom. London, 1947.
    (e) Sir J. Chadwick: Atomic Energy. London, 1947.
    (f) Sir John Cockcroft: Nuclear Power. London, 1947.
58. (a) Harwell, The British atomic energy research establishment, 1946-51, London, 1952.
    (b) The British Atomic Commission. Britain's Atomic Factories. London, 1954. 100 pages, very important.
59. F. Joliot-Curie: L'énergie atomique en France. *Atomes*, Paris, June 1947, and La science atomique au sevice de la mort. *Démocratie nouvelle*, Paris, May 1948.
60. J. Guéron: Energie nucléaire et politique générale. *Atomes*, Paris, July 1947, and Aspects économiques et internationaux de l'énergie atomique. *Génie civil*, Paris, August 15, 1947.
61. E. Biörklund: Comment limiter les armes atomiques? *Revue des deux Mondes*, June 1954.
62. Rapport Annuel, Institut Interuniversitaire des Sciences Nucléaires, Brussels, 1952-54.

---

63. Balchaja Sovjetskaja Entsiklopedia. Moscow, 1950. 80 pages, important. Part 31 published in 1955: 10 pages.
64. Periodicals such as *Doklady*, *Vjestnik*, *Acta Fysikochimika*, *Biochimija*, and *Priroda;* interesting, some of them important.
65. Atvjety tavarischtscha Stalina, *Pravda*, Moscow, October 30, 1946.
66. Zapis besjedy Stalina, *Pravda*, Moscow, May 8, 1947.

67. *Pravda*, Moscow, November 7, 1947.
68. Speech by Gromyko, *New York Times*, May 20, 1947.
69. Mechdunarodny absor, *Pravda*, Moscow, June 24 and October 11, 1948.
70. Kto che sryvajet ustanovlenije kontrol? (Who prevents control?) *Pravda*, Moscow, June 1948.
71. *Pravda*, Moscow: 25 articles in October and 7 in November 1948.
72. Ten articles by M. Rubenstein in the newspaper *Trudj* and *New Times*, Moscow, with an analysis of the book, 'One World or None' and a critical review of America's policy. June 1946-August 1948.
73. V kommisiji OON po kontrolio nad atomnoj energiej (in the UN Atomic Energy Commission), *Pravda*, Moscow, April 11 and May 13, 1948.
74. U. Zhukov. Udar po atomnoj diplomatii (Bad luck to atomic diplomacy), *Pravda*, Moscow, October 4, 1948.
75. Newspapers *Robotnik* and *Przeglad Miedzy-narodovy*, Warsaw, June-September 1948.
76. (a) TASS communications in *Soviet Monitor*, London, September 25, 1949.
    (b) E. M. Zacharias: Behind Closed Doors. New York, 1951.
77. Speeches at the 32nd anniversary of the October Revolution, *Pravda*, Moscow, November 7, 1949.
78. Speech by Voroshilov at Minsk. *Izvestia*, Moscow, March 8, 1950.
79. Speech by Molotov, *Pravda*, Moscow, March 11, 1950.
80. Election speech by Kaganovich, *Pravda*, Moscow, March 11, 1950.
81. Zajavlenije Verchovnavo Sovjeta SSSR (Declaration by the USSR Supreme Council), *Pravda*, Moscow, June 21, 1950.
82. Professor E. Tarle asks whether the fact that Russia has the atomic bomb will not change the attitude of the USA.
83. I. Viktorov: Atomny tupik (The Atomic Hatchet), *Pravda*, July 25, 1949.
84. Articles in *Izvestia*, Moscow, March 21, 1950.
85. M. Inosemtsev: Militarisatsyia naoky v SSHA (Militarization of Science in the USA), *Izvestia*, Moscow, April 13, 1950.
86. M. Rubenstein, *New Times*, Moscow, April 9, 1951.
87. Atvjet predstavitelya SSSR v OON (Reply from Soviet's representative to the UN), *Pravda*, Moscow, September 27, 1950.

APPENDIX I

88. *Pravda*, Moscow, November 26, December 9 and April 22, 1951.
89. Besjeda tavarischtscha Stalina (Interview with Comrade Stalin), *Izvestia*, Moscow, February 17, 1951.
90. Atvjet tavarischtscha Stalina (Reply from Comrade Stalin), *Pravda*, Moscow, October 6, 1951.
91. G. M. Malenkov: Atchotnyi doklad XIX Siesda partii (Explanatory Report to the 19th Party Congress), *Pravda*, Moscow, October 6, 1952.
92. E. Biörklund: The New Russian Government, *Svensk Tidskrift* No. 9, 1953.
93. E. Biörklund: The liberation policy in the satellite states, *Svensk Tidskrift* No. 2, 1954.
94. *Ost-Probleme*, January 1954 and *Osteuropa*, February 1954.
95. The sources are Russian newspapers and periodicals (see 64), articles in *Tjassovoj*, *Russkaja Myisl*, and many articles in American and English periodicals.
96. American Review of the Soviet Union, New York 1946—Articles by G. Oster and other writers about Soviet atomic problems.
97. Gordon Dean: Report on the Atom. London 1954, Chapter XIV; this book has rather few names and facts about Russia. The conclusions regarding the atomic energy situation in the Soviet are very interesting.
98. W. Gordon East. The new frontiers of the Soviet Union, *Foreign Affairs*, July 1951. Soviet expansion and new Russian treaties; interesting.
99. Balchaja Sovjetskaja Entsiklopedija, Moscow 1950. Articles on all satellite states; important source.
100. Statesman's Year Book, 1954.
101. Y. Gluckstein: Stalin's Satellites in Europe. London, George Allen & Unwin 1952. Economic and social conditions, how the Russian state is built up. 333 pages, very important.
102. Articles in newspapers and periodicals from the satellite states 1952-54.
103. Articles in Eastern German newspapers (cf. 94 above).
104. Speeches by Khruschev and others, *Pravda* and *Izvestia* 1953-54.
105. J. Wszelaki: The rise of industrial Middle Europe, *Foreign Affairs*, October 1951. Important though finished in 1951.
106. E. Lemberg: Osteuropa und die Sovjetunion. Stuttgart 1950. Describes the different races in Eastern Europe; interesting from a psychological point of view.

INTERNATIONAL ATOMIC POLICY

107. Zelda K. Coates: Soviet in Central Asia. New York 1952. Information on Kazakstan, Tadzhikistan, Turkmenistan, Uzbekistan and Kirgisia; mentions some uranium mines.
108. M. Fainsod: How Russia is Ruled. Cambridge 1953. 575 pages, important.
109. L. B. Schapiro: The Post-War Treaties of the Soviet Union, The Year Book of World Affairs, 1950; interesting.
110. L. Deutscher: Russia—What Next? London 1953.

SPECIAL LITERATURE (in addition to that already mentioned) dealing with deposits of uranium, thorium and lithium.

111. W. van Royen and O. Bowles: The Mineral Resources of the World, New York 1952-54.
112. E. Kohl: Uran. Stuttgart 1954. Very important standard work, but with few data on the Eastern Powers. 234 pages. Must be supplemented by information cited in 64, 95, 96, 97, 99, 107 above and 114 below.
113. *Engineering and Mining Journal*. New York 1952-54.
114. *Mining World*. Washington 1951-53. Very important. Special articles by D. B. Shimkin (born in Russia), the metallurgical specialist. He has also written: Minerals—a Key to Soviet Power. Harvard 1951; important.
115. Report of the Geological Survey Board. London 1950 and following.
116. Glückauf, *Bergmännische Zeitschrift*, Essen 1954.
117. *Tidsskrift för Kjemi, Bergwesen og Metallurgi*, Oslo 1952-54.
118. (a) The Mining Survey, Transvaal, 1952-54, on South Africa.
    (b) Western Miner, Vancouver, November 1954, on the new uranium fields at Blind River (Algoma).
    (c) R. D. Nininger: Minerals for Atomic Energy. New York, December 1954. A standard work on where fissionable materials are to be found. Maps far from complete.

SPECIAL LITERATURE ON CHINA

119. M. Beloff: Soviet Policy in the Far East. Oxford 1951. Important for period 1944-51; 278 pages.
120. Mao-Tsé-Toung (Mao Tse-tung): La stratégie de la Guerre révolutionnaire en Chine. Paris 1950.
121. C. M. Chang. Five Years of Communist Rule in China, *Foreign Affairs*, October 1954; important.
122. F. Leprince-Ringuet: L'Avenir de l'Asie Russe. Paris 1951.

APPENDIX I

123. R. C. North: Moscow and Chinese Communists. Stanford University Press 1953.
124. W. Kolarz: The Peoples of the Soviet Far East. New York 1954.
125. Russian and Chinese notes, October 1954.
126. *People's China*, No. 15, 1954.
127. H. W. Baldwin: China as a military power, *Foreign Affairs*, October 1951.
128. B. Rigg: Red China's Fighting Hordes. Harrisburg 1951.
129. Adlai E. Stevenson: Korea in perspective, *Foreign Affairs*, April 1952.
130. *People's China*, No. 20, 1954.
131. Dr H. R. Wei: International Control of Atomic Energy. Translated and published in New York 1948-50.

---

132. USA Department of State. Atomic Energy, October 1946. Interesting on what was done during the war 1939-45.
133. United Nations, General Assembly, Doc. A/C. I/L 105 Rev 1/54.
134. ,, ,, ,, ,, Doc. A/C. 1/759/54.
135. ,, ,, ,, ,, Doc. A/2818/54.
136. ,, ,, ,, ,, Doc. A/C. 5/L. 312/54 and A/2820/54.

Altogether 200 sources are mentioned here.

APPENDIX 2

Important Deposits of Fissionable Material

Small deposits are not mentioned in the following table, for that would have made both the table and the map too large. Uranium, thorium, lithium and so on may be obtained from more than 200 different kinds of ore, and many mines yield two or more of these materials. For that reason it was found expedient not to use different symbols for different kinds of deposits.

The table and the map should be studied together, and to facilitate this the map is made to open out of the book.

Experience has shown that if a map is made of the large deposits and the symbols placed in their geographical positions, a small map would be difficult to read, and would not give a picture of the relative importance of production. Circles of different sizes do not give the same clear impression. For that reason the map is made according to the principle that symbols for deposits—blue dots for deposits belonging to the Western Powers, red for the Eastern Powers and green for others—are placed in the neighbourhood of their geographical positions, and in the case of a very rich deposit the dots are grouped round a centre. This gives a picture of the relative extent of fissionable material in a country, but the exact positions of the deposits are not shown. The map is not intended as a geological or metallurgical one, but to make it possible for the reader to judge of the feasibility of controlling atomic energy, and other political problems. Less rich deposits are marked with a cross.

In the table, the Western Powers come first and after that, pages 146-148, the Eastern Powers. Other powers and smaller states are at the foot. There is much contradictory information about the production capacity of Russian mines, but it has been possible to get an approximately correct picture from the literature available. It is much more difficult to get reliable figures for the capacity of each group of mines, and an important reservation must be made for these. But they give a rather good idea of the total production. The special literature that has been used seems to show that the following production figures in tons of uranium ore per day are probably correct (for comparison the figures have been reduced to the same uranium content, 0.28 per cent):

APPENDIX 2

Western Powers		Dots on map	Eastern Powers		Dots on map
USA	24,000	62	Soviet	20,000	46
Belgian Congo*	16,000	36*	Eastern Germany, Czechoslovakia	1,000-2,000(?)	5
Canada	12,000	31			
South Africa	8,000	20			
Great Britain, France, Western Germany	2,000	5	Poland and Bulgaria	1,000	3
Australia	2,000-4,000	7	Sinkiang, Manchuria, Northern Korea	4,000(?)	9
			People's Republic of China	2,000(?)	6

Total about 65,000 tons per day
 ,,   ,,   720 deposits

Total about 28,000 tons per day
 ,,   ,,   300 deposits

This shows that 93,000 tons of ore are produced daily, which makes about 34,000,000 tons a year, if only the above mentioned countries are counted. The Western Powers utilize about 70 per cent, and the Eastern Powers about 30 per cent of the whole.

The positions of the atomic factories are not marked, for that would give the map military importance, and that is not the aim. The USA has published far more about factories than has the Soviet. This does not signify that there is not an extensive literature on Soviet uranium mines, but there is naturally no official Russian confirmation.

Country	Large Minefields	Approx. number of mines
USA—contd.	Colorado Plateau, 18 minefields with 290 mines (only 19 marked in map). Best known are Salt Wash, Shinarump, Chinte, Moenkopi. Also minefields in south-west (Powder River, Haystack), north (Idaho-Montana) and east USA and Alaska.	

*Although the deposits are situated in the south-eastern corner of the Belgian Congo, the dots are placed in the north in order to avoid placing them in Rhodesia.

INTERNATIONAL ATOMIC POLICY

Country	Large Minefields	Approx. number of mines
USA	The best-known atomic plants (factories, atomic piles, experimental stations, but not laboratories) are: in California, San Francisco, in Colorado, Grand Junction and Rocky Flats, in Delaware, Wilmington, in Georgia, Savannah River, in Idaho, Idaho Falls, in Illinois, Chicago, in Indiana, Dana, in Iowa, Ames and Burlington, in Kentucky, Paducah, in Long Island, Brookhaven, in Missouri, Kansas City and St. Louis, in Nevada, Las Vegas, in New Mexico, Eniwetok, Los Alamos, Sandia and Santa Fé, in New York State, West Milton and Schenectady, in Ohio, Cleveland, Dayton, Fernald, Lockland and Portsmouth, in Pennsylvania, Pittsburgh, in Tennessee, Oak Ridge, in Texas, Pantex and in the State of Washington, Hanford and Richland. The whole of the USA is divided into atomic energy districts, and a central organ is in charge of problems of organization. The most important atomic factories are directly subordinate to the US Atomic Energy Commission in Washington. (All information taken from the official reports of the Commission.)	530 mines, of which 62 are marked on map
Belgian Congo	In that Katanga District of the Elisabethville minefields at Shinkolobwe, one of the richest mines in the world, and at Ruashi, Luiswichi, Kalongwe, etc. Also cobalt mines.	About 30 large mines
Canada	Saskatchewan (Athabaska) enormously rich and often called 'the Uranium Hot Spot', and Port Radium (Eldorado). Also mines in western Canada (Cariboo Hill), and southern Canada. There is cobalt in Canada, too.	About 40 mines, some large

APPENDIX 2

Country	Large Minefields	Approx. number of mines
South Africa	In Transvaal at Johannesburg (12 mines) and in the Orange Free State 10 large gold mines; uranium is extracted from the waste. Very rich mines (12) at Witwatersrand. Also mines in Rhodesia, Tanganyika, Mozambique (Tete) and Swakopmund. Cobalt in North Rhodesia.	About 35 mines
Great Britain and British Commonwealth	In the Tavistock district of Cornwall and in Devon at least 12 mines, including Gunnislake, Bedford, Dartmoor and Standon Hill. In Australia, Rum Jungle (north), Radium Hill (Mount Painter, Olary) in the south and Port Hedland in the north-west. Mines in New Zealand and Ceylon. Atomic factories in England: Springfields, Windscale with a pipeline out into the sea, for atomic ash, and Capenhurst. Harwell is the centre for atomic research. Canada—see above.	About 30 mines
France	Round Puy-de-Dôme about 20 mines, in the Vosges, Nogent-sur-Marne, Saint-Denis. Also in Madagascar and in French Morocco 6 mines. Cobalt in Morocco. Atomic plants at Saclay, Chatillon and Le Bouchet.	About 35 mines

Note 1. It was learned at the beginning of 1955 that the uranium sources of Canada had been considerably increased. The 'Blind River Uranium Field', by the Great Lakes (see Appendix 3), called the 'Billion Dollar Camp', at Algoma and the surroundings, is expected to produce about 12,000 tons of uranium ore a day during 1955, and is calculated to contain between 12 and 15 million tons of uranium ore. These deposits are greater than those of the Eldorado Mine, and perhaps those of Saskatchewan. Blind River is marked on the map with a large blue circle.

INTERNATIONAL ATOMIC POLICY

Country	Large Minefields	Approx. number of mines
Western Germany	In Schwarzwald and the Vosges about 20 mines, all small ones. A few mines in north-eastern Bavaria.	About 20 mines
Soviet	The large minefields lie along the south border of Siberia and in the gold mines of Siberia, but there are deposits in other places. The name 'Atomgrad' indicates large minefields or atomic plants or both in combination. In North Karelia: Poljarnikrug, Chitoostrov, Tjarnaja Salmo (by the White Sea), etc., in Estonia are the shale mines Jojvi and Kotla, in Caucasia there are several mines (4?) and 'Atomgrad 1'. In Ukraine, to the north-east of Lake Asovska are some mines. In the Urals north of Magnitogorsk is 'Atomgrad 2' with 10 partly new mines (also cobalt). In the Pamir Plateau in north-eastern Afghanistan is 'Atomgrad 3' with about 10 mines. In the rich Ferghana district, north of Pamir and south of Andishan are some 10 large mines. There are also mines, etc., at Alma Ata, south of Lake Balkasch and at Tannu Tuva (Atomgrad 4?). Its situation is given in different places by several specialists, but it seems to be north-east of Lake Balkasch	About 200 mines, possibly more

Note 2. In addition there are other countries with deposits of varying size: Belgium (Vielsalm), Denmark, a mine in Greenland (King Oscar's Fjord), Norway (Glanfjord, Evje and other places), atomic pile at Kjeller, north of Oslo, Sweden (Kvarntorp), Italy, five small mines, Portugal (Port Urgeirica in the north), Switzerland, a few small mines, Spain (3), Mexico (4), Malacca (2), Sumatra (3), Borneo (2-4), Brazil (8), Japan (4) and India about 10 newly-discovered deposits, particularly thorium. A total of about 50 mines.

APPENDIX 2

Country	Large Minefields	Approx. number of mines
Soviet	near Kolgon. There is a minefield near Lake Baikal in Siberia, as in Transbaikal and the coastal belt by the Sea of Japan (Styjudjansk), in the Sajan Mountains and the Aldan Mountains, in gold mines at Kolymsk, Vjerchojansk and north of Anadyr by the Bering Sea. In addition there are several mines in Kirgisia, Turkmenistan and Tadzhikistan east of the Caspian Sea. Atomic plants at Atomgrad 1-4 and an unknown number in connection with certain mines.	
Soviet's satellite states	Eastern Germany has about 20 mines: in German Saxony, Breitenbrunn (St Christoph), Altenberg, Freiberg, Zinnwald, Chemnitz, Zwickau, Annaberg, Schneeberg, Johanngeorgenstadt. Ten of these are worked by the Russian War Office.	20
	Czechoslovakia has 45 mines. Four large mines at St Joachimsthal (Jachymov), worked by a Russian company ('Wismut') with 100,000 German workmen, and 35,000 Russian troops to guard them; Teplitz Schönau (1), Schönficht (2), Becken (26), Isergebirge (8) and Adlergebirge (2); (Schlaggenwald is in Bohemia).	45
	In West Sinkiang (south of Tannu Tuva) there are Russian mines and atomic plants at Thiwa. The Soviet works the mine Whanghai in North Korea. A minefield at Lysa Gora in Poland, one at Gotenburg in Bulgaria north of Sofia, and at Stara Zagora near Varna.	15

Country	Large Minefields	Approx. number of mines
People's Republic of China	There are mines where uranium and lithium are produced in the provinces of Kwangsi, Hunan, Kiangsi, East Kwangsi, in the Tachim Mountains and south Manchuria. Altogether about 20 mines. The atomic industry is undeveloped.	20

For Product Safety Concerns and Information please contact our EU representative GPSR@taylorandfrancis.com
Taylor & Francis Verlag GmbH, Kaufingerstraße 24, 80331 München, Germany

www.ingramcontent.com/pod-product-compliance
Lightning Source LLC
Chambersburg PA
CBHW052129300426
44116CB00010B/1837